Mastering
Apple Watch
Series 9

Your Essential Guide to Effortless Mastery of Apple Watch Series 9

Fritsche King

TABLE OF CONTENTS

INTRODUCTION

The Apple Watch can be described as a line of smartwatches developed by Apple Inc. It adds fitness tracking, health-oriented capabilities, and wireless telecommunication, integrating with iOS and other Apple products and services. The Apple Watch was produced initially in April 2015 and swiftly became the best-selling wearable device. About 4.2 million pieces were sold in the second quarter of fiscal 2015, and, not more than 2015 million people were said to be users of an Apple Watch as of December 2022. Apple Watch has brought about a new generation of the Apple Watch with more improved internal components labeled by Apple as a series with some exceptions. Each of the Apple Series has been sold before in lots of variants defined by the watch casing's material, color, and size except the Series 1 and SE which are available just in aluminum, and the Ultra-available in 49 mm uncolored titanium, and commencing with Series 3, by the option in the aluminum variants for LTE cellular connectivity, which are almost of the same standard with all other materials. The band that was included with the watch can be selected from various options from Apple, and watch variants in aluminum co-branded with Nike, and in stainless steel also co-branded with Hermes are also provided, which also has exclusive brands, colors, and digital watch faces displaying the branding of those companies.

The Apple Watch works alongside the user's iPhone for functions like configuring the watch and syncing data with the applications in the user's iPhone, but it can be connected separately to a Wi-Fi network for data-reliant purposes, and can also make and receive phone calls on its own when the iPhone paired with it is not close or is switched off, thereby offering a reduced need for an iPhone initial configuration. The oldest iPhone model can be used with any Apple Watch based on the version of system software that has been installed on each of the devices (both the phone and the watch). As of September 2022, new Apple Watches are already installed with WatchOS 9 and need an iPhone that runs on iOS 16, which can be found in iPhone 8 and other versions released after it. Apple Watch runs the WatchOS whose interface is dependent on a home screen with circular app icons, which can be altered to a list view in the configurations of the device (usually at the discretion of the user). The OS can be navigated with the use of the touchscreen of the crown on the side of the watch. While Apple was unveiling this, the first set of the Watch Series was paired with the iPhone 5 or phones made later that were running iOS 8.2 or later, this version of iOS introduced the Apple Watch app, which is often used for the pairing of the watch with an iPhone, configure settings and loaded applications, and also display applications from the App Store that are compatible. The Apple Watch can receive notifications, messages, and phone calls when synced with an iPhone. "Glances" allows users to swipe between pages with widget-like information displays, but this functionality was superseded by a redesigned Control Center. watchOS now enables Handoff, which allows Apple Watch to send content to an iOS or macOS device and act as a viewfinder for an iPhone camera. Siri is also accessible for voice commands and can reply with voice prompts on Series 3 watches. Apple Watch additionally accepts Apple Pay, allowing it to be used with older iPhone models that lack near-field communication (NFC) capabilities. The built-in iOS apps on the Apple Watch, including Stocks, Wallet, Mail, Phone, Calendar, Messages, Music, Photos, Reminders, and Remote (which can manage iTunes and Apple TV), are intended to work together. The Activity and Workout apps allow users to monitor their physical activity and send data back to their iPhones for use in the health app and other HealthKit-compatible applications. With watchOS 3, the stock apps now include Reminders, Home, Find My Friends, Heart Rate, and Breathe.

There are also third-party applications that run in the Watch OS. For instance, in WatchOS 1, third-party WatchKit applications were being executed in the background on the iPhone as an application extension while native user interface resources were installed on the Apple Watch. Hence, watchOS applications ought to be implemented within their iOS application and will then be synced to the watch either manually or automatically when the phone installation is being carried out. With the release of WatchOS 2, Apple ensured it became compulsory for new watch applications to be produced with the watchOS 2 SDK from June 1, 2016, onwards; no third-party languages or SDKs can be used in the development of the applications. This enabled developers to design native applications that are being executed on the watch itself, hence bringing an improvement to the responsiveness of third-party applications. In Watch 05 and earlier, all the applications of watchOS are regarded as dependent applications; the WatchOS application relies on an iOS companion application to function well. In watchOS 6 or later, developers can now design independent watchOS applications, and it no longer needs an application to be installed on the iPhone paired with the watch. This was aided by the introduction of a different App Store on the Apple Watch itself.

Welcome to the Apple Watch Series 9

As of September 2023, about ten different generations and ten series of Apple Watch have been released. Apple Watch models have been split into about five different collections; Apple Watch (1st generation), Apple Watch Sport (1st generation), Apple Watch Nike + (Series 2-present), Apple Watch Hermes (1st generation-Series 5, Series 6-present), and Apple Watch Edition (1st generation-Series 3, Series 5, Series 6- present). They are differentiated via the combinations of cases, bands, and exclusive watch faces; Apple Watch as earlier stated comes with either aluminum or stainless steel cases, and diverse watch bands; Apple Watch Hermès uses stainless steel cases and Hermès leather watch bands (also included is an exclusive Hermès orange sport band); Apple Watch Nike+ uses aluminum cases and Nike sport bands or sport loops; Apple Watch Edition uses ceramic cases and a variety of bands (the first generation Apple Watch Edition used 18 karat yellow or rose gold). Series 5 introduced a new titanium casing to the Edition tier.Apple Watch Series 1 models were formerly available with just aluminum cases and sports bands. As of Series 3, each Apple Watch model is in aluminum, the least expensive casing is available either with or without the use of LTE cellular connectivity, while the models with the other casing materials available (stainless steel and times ceramic and titanium) always have it.

Each model through Series 3 comes in a 38-or 42- millimeter body, with the larger size having a mildly larger screen and battery. Series 4 has also been updated to 40- and 44-millimeter models respectively. Each model has diverse color and band options. Featured Apple-designed bands have colored sports bands, sport loops, woven nylon bands, classic buckles, modern buckles, leather loops, Milanese loops, and link bracelets.

What's New in Series 9

Introducing the Apple Watch Series 9 which happens to be the latest Apple Watch boasts of the new S9 SiP chip, which allows for a much brighter display and ensures it is much easier than ever for a lost iPhone to be located with Precision Finding for iPhone. In this section, you will learn about the new features that come with this new release and also how you can get the best from these features.

Updated Interface

Apple Watch is now much easier to use. This can be attributed to an updated interface that takes complete advantage of the display of the Apple Watch and offers a lot more information at one glance. WatchOS 10 provides redesigned applications, Smart Stack, and diverse ways for navigation.

Introducing the Smart Stack

With this new feature, you will be able to get all of the information you need, just where you need it from any interface at all. All you have to do is get the Digital Crown turned to show widgets in the Smart Start. The Smart Stack can be described as a set of widgets that makes use of information like time, location, and the various activities you get involved in to instantly show the most relevant widgets in due time during your day. For instance, when you just start the day, Weather will display the forecast, or when you are going from one place to another, the Smart Stack will display boarding passes from Wallet.

To open the Smart Stack;

- Tap the **Digital Crown** to display the face of the watch if it is not showing yet.
- Switch the **Digital Crown** to move down until you are able to see widgets.

- Move down **to the widget** you would like to make use of, then touch it to get its associated application opened.

At the lower part of the Smart Stack, you will see a widget that has three featured applications which are Music, Workouts, and Messages. Touch any application of your choice to get it opened.

To add, remove, and rearrange widgets;

Widgets that are already included in the Smart Stack can be manually added, removed, and rearranged. To perform any of the following actions, simply scroll down from the watch face, touch, and hold the Smart Stack.

- **Add a widget:** Touch +, then touch **a featured widget** or touch an application that shows underneath All Applications. Some applications provide more than just one widget.

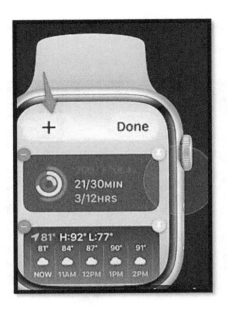

- **Remove a widget**: Touch **the red circle** with the - icon embedded in it.

- **Pin and unpin widgets**: Touch **the pin icon** on the right side of the widget. The pinned widget will then be displayed underneath the last pinned widget in the Smart Stack. If you would like to move the widget to the upper part of the stack, unpin the widgets over it by tapping **the icon on the right side** of each of the widgets.

When you are done modifying the Smart Stack, touch **Done**.

New ways to open the Control Center and show your most recently used applications

To get this done, all you have to do is tap the side button in order to have the Control Center opened from the watch face or just any other application.

- Touch the **Digital Crown twice to show the App Switcher.**

Using the Control Center on Apple Watch

Control Center offers you quite an easy way to check your battery, get your watch silenced, pick a Focus, change your Apple Watch into a flashlight, place your Apple Watch in Airplane Mode, switch on theater mode, and lots more.

- **Open Control Center**: Tap the **side button just once.**
- **Close Control Center**: Ensure the **Control Center is open**, move your wrist away from you or you can choose to tap t**he side button once more.**

There are very small icons at the upper part of the Control Center that show the status or some configurations. For instance, it can show that your Apple Watch is connected to cellular, your location is being utilized by an application, and that features such as Airplane Mode and Do Not Disturb are turned on. If you would like to check the status icons, tap the side button to open **the Control Center.** If you would like more details. Touch **the various icons** on the screen. You are not condemned to using the Control Center at its default stage, you can choose to modify the Control Center to suit your taste.

If you would like to rearrange the buttons in Control Center by following the steps below;

- Touch **the side button** to get the Control Center opened.
- Navigate **to the lower part of the Control Center**.
- Tap and hold **a button**, then move it to another location.
- Touch **Done** when you are through with this.

Furthermore, you can choose to take off the buttons in the Control Center by following these steps;

- Touch **the side buttons** to open the **Control Center**.
- Navigate **to the button** of the Control Center, then touch **Edit.**

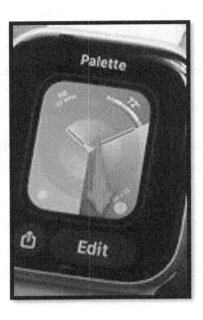

- Touch **the red circle** which is usually located in the corner of the button you would like to take off.
- Touch **Done** when you are through.

If you would like to bring back a button you removed perhaps if the removal was done by mistake,

- Open Control Center, touch **Edit**, then touch the green icon in the corner of the button you would like to restore. Touch **Done** when you are through!

You can also choose to make use of the App Switcher in the opening of applications on your watch. The App Switcher grants you swift access to the applications you have used recently. The Home Screen can show applications in a grid or list view. When you first configure your Apple Watch, you make a choice of the view you would like to have.

Follow the steps below to have this view changed;

- From the watch face, touch the **Digital crown** to display the Home screen.
- Make use of the **Digital Crown to navigate to the lower part of the screen**, then pick **Grid View or List View**.

You can also choose to open the Settings app, touch App View, and then pick Gridview or Listview.

To open an application from the App Switcher, follow the steps below;

- Click twice on **the Digital Crown**, then use the Digital Crown to move through the applications you have used in recent times. It is worth noting that applications that are currently executing a session; a map navigation session or a workout session, for instance, will be displayed at the top of the list of the applications.
- Touch **an application to get it opened**.

Explore new watch faces

Get things livened up with the use of the new watch faces for the Apple Watch. Here you will have Snoopy the Peanuts character, interact with Woodstock known as his feathered friend, and the hands of the watch; Solar Analog helps with the lighting up at night so that its legibility will be quite enhanced and also helps with the creation of a dramatic effect. The Palette shows the time as a range of beautiful colors that move all through the day.

Hit the trail

Here you can make use of Maps to look up and learn crucial information about nearby trails in the United States, such as name, duration, time, photographs, and more. Download topographic maps and other offline maps.

New Compass elevation and waypoint features

On the Apple Watch Series 9, you can view waypoint elevations in relation to your present location and receive notifications when you've surpassed a certain elevation. You can also view waypoints that indicate when you were last able to make an Emergency SOS call or establish a cellular connection.

Enhanced Cycling workouts

The time is now to pedal while wearing an Apple Watch. Automatically add cadence and power measurements to your workout display by connecting to Bluetooth-enabled gear. Check out estimates of your functional threshold power, which is the most intense amount of activity you are capable of for an hour. When you begin a cycling workout from your watch, it instantly appears as a Live Activity on your iPhone. It will take over the entire display when you tap it, making it simpler to see your data while riding.

Fitness+ Improvements

Custom Plans can help Apple Fitness+ customers work out more frequently. Choose the days, workout styles, durations, trainers, and music that work best for you, and Fitness+ will develop a Custom Plan to help you stay on track. Additionally, you can now stack various exercises and meditations to transition smoothly to your next task.

Locate Friends with the use of Live Locations

Locate buddies nearby in real-time. Is a friend who was supposed to meet you for lunch late? Find out where they are and when they expect to arrive by checking in. A Messages chat where you've shared your location will allow it to update in real-time.

Log your state of mind

Select how you're feeling after scrolling through eye-catching graphics to record your current emotions and mood for the day. Keep your watch face's complications and alerts consistent.

Set time spent in daylight

Nearsightedness, or myopia, usually develops during childhood. Encourage your youngster to spend more time outdoors during the day as an approach to help lower the danger. Now, the Apple Watch's ambient light sensor can determine the time during the day. Parents can monitor it with Family Setup even if their youngster doesn't have an iPhone.

Getting the Most from Your Apple Watch Experience

Beyond just how sleek it looks; the Apple Watch Series 9 is great at helping you remain on top of real-time happenings all around the world. With this watch, you can become quite focused on very important things and not have the need to reach out for your phone almost every time as it helps to notify you of the very important digital events immediately they happen and also enables you to act on them immediately without any need to grab your phone. Running checks on your text messages and emails all by quickly checking your watch helps to save so much time and save so much more when you are engaged in an important activity. If you have owned an Apple Watch before, I would say you are used to taking calls on it, pinging your iPhone anytime you cannot locate it, tracking your workouts, and checking your notifications right on your wrist while your phone doesn't leave your pocket. All of these are amazing but then there is so much more your Apple Watch can do as a mini version of your iPhone.

Control the iPhone Camera

The Apple Watch is able to control the camera of your iPhone especially when it has to do with you taking pictures. One of the applications on the Apple Watch is just like the camera on the iPhone. Once you open the application, the camera on your phone will also come on. The application has a three-second timer by default hence it doesn't look as though you are touching your watch in that selfie.

All you have to do is get your iPhone propped on a table or shelf, or a tripod if there is a need for you to get quite fancy. With that, you are completely ready to gain control of the camera remotely. To locate the camera app on your Apple Watch simply navigate through your applications by touching down on the digital crown then pick the one that has the camera icon. This will then open the camera on your iPhone and display a preview of what the camera can see on the display of your watch. You are at liberty to make a choice from the front or rear camera right from your watch. You are also free to make use of other options like Flash, Live Photo, and HDR. When you touch down the shutter button, you will commence the recording of a video.

Automatic hand-washing timer

The importance of washing hands can never be overemphasized especially with the outbreak of Covid19. To help us cultivate the habit of washing our hands, the Apple Watch Series 9 is able to detect instantly when you commence the washing of your hands. It will then commence a 20-second countdown, vibrating when the time is completed. If you do not already wash for the recommended 20 seconds, this is a very nice tool that can help you start.

Apple Maps on your Watch

It is imperative that you use Apple Maps if you frequently require directions and own an Apple Watch. Your Apple Watch functions optimally when paired with Apple's exclusive navigation app, in true ecosystem form. When using step-by-step navigation, you can use the Apple Watch to search for directions. You will also receive haptic feedback when you need to make a turn or leave. If you live in a major city and walk a lot, this feature is quite useful. Look down at your phone for turn-by-turn directions to prevent being sidetracked. Additionally, if you frequently miss turns and exits regardless of the navigation program you use, this can help you avoid driving while preoccupied. As the Apple Watch doesn't vibrate in different ways to notify you to make a right or left turn, but rather vibrates when you need to take an action, keep in mind that this is more of a guide than a replacement for GPS navigation. Unless you have earbuds in to hear the voice direction at the other end, you would still need to look down at your watch to determine what to do.

Sleep Schedule

The Apple Watch is an amazing sleep tracker. It has the capability to track sleep stages and cycles with very appropriate accuracy, especially for a device that is worn on the wrist. Making use of it alongside your sleep schedule on your iPhone is even more of a greater use. The Health app has various sleep options. In this place, you are able to see some of all the sleep data from previous nights and also alter your sleep schedule. When you include a sleep schedule from 11:15 p.m. to 6:15 a.m., this means you will get reminders to commence winding down each night from around 10:30 p.m. The sleep focus will come on immediately each day during your 'sleep' times on both your phone and your watch after which you can then configure an alarm for each morning. Personally, making use of the Apple Watch for the use of my alarm alone has helped me in many ways especially when it has to do with getting up in the mornings since vibration can be felt on my wrist each morning as against an audible alarm that can keep the whole house awake especially if you are not staying alone.

Calculator

If you happen to be dining out and have a need to calculate your tips very fast, all you have to do is open the Apple Watch application, insert the bill amount, choose Tip, and then have your watch calculate the amount. You can also choose to alter tip percentages, see both the tip amount and total amount in the calculator. You can also choose to add a number of people to split the amount with.

Find your iPhone with Ease

Whenever you have your friends around, you can always trust that one of them will pick up your phone. They may either have a need to take pictures, surf the net, or watch movies. When this is ongoing, you may be looking for your phone in the process. You can use your watch to ping your phone with ease. This will help you reduce the number of hours you would have spent searching for your phone.

Walkie-Talkie

The rooms in my home are all divided and largely walled off, so I used to joke that we'd need an intercom system from the 1970s to interact with one another when I first moved in. However, the Walkie-Talkie feature on the Apple Watch provided the solution. You can use your watches to communicate in real-time with everyone else in your home who has an Apple Watch.

Apple Pay on Your Wrist

As a contactless payment method, employing Apple Pay on your iPhone is already a fantastic feature. However, using your Apple Watch to check out at the register without even having to take your phone out of your purse or pockets is even better. It works even if you don't have your iPhone with you.

Lastly, even though the Apple Watch has quite a smaller screen than a normal phone, there are a lot of games that can be played on it. Although they appear to be much simpler than the games obtainable on phones, you can however still play them. The process to get a game for your Apple Watch is the same as searching for applications. All you have to do is go to the App Store and find the games that are available.

Overview of This Book

This unique book has been carefully written to ensure that you learn how that is unnecessary and be able to make the most of your Apple Watch Series 9. Below are some of the exciting things you will get to learn in this book;

Chapter 1: Unboxing and Initial Setup

This is the first chapter after the introduction and it contains all you need to know after you've unboxed your Apple Watch. In this chapter, you will learn about charging your watch and how to manage power on it. Furthermore, you will learn how to pair your watch with your iPhone for proper usage, and configure cellular and family setup and you will also learn about watch faces and how best to customize it.

Change 2: Navigating Your Apple Watch

Here in this chapter, you will learn more about the use of the Apple Watch, getting into every corner of the watch. In this chapter, you will learn about the hardware components, the use of the digital crown and the side button as well as making use of the various touchscreen gestures.

Chapter 3: Personalizing Your Watch Face

There is nothing as amazing as having your watch just look the way you want and not how Apple has customized it to be. In this chapter, you will learn about the customization of the watch face and get to know more about complications (this is not the English meaning but just a term used by Apple). You will also learn about time travel and timekeeping enhancements, the use of alarms, timers, and world clocks. This chapter has so much to offer to ensure that you get the best out of your Apple Watch.

Chapter 4: Staying Connected

Your watch can help you remain connected to the world as just your phone would. In this chapter, you will learn about the use of the notification center, making calls on your Apple watch, sending messages, and managing email and other third-party messaging applications.

Chapter 5: Health and Fitness Mastery

One major benefit of the Apple Watch Series 9 over all other smartwatches is the fact that it helps to contribute positively to ensuring that you remain healthy and fit. In this chapter, you will learn about the various applications that can help ensure that you remain healthy like ECG and Blood Oxygen monitoring applications, Heart Health monitoring applications, and lots more.

Chapter 6: Enhancing Your Experience with Apps

Another fun thing about the use of the Apple Watch Series 9 is the fact that you can also make use of applications and even download some from the App Store just like you would with your iPhone. In this chapter, you will learn about some of the built-in apps you can access on your watch, you will learn about how to customize glance and dock, and also how you can multitask on your watch.

Chapter 7: Music, Media, and Beyond

In this chapter, you will learn about the use of iTunes on your Apple watch. You will also learn how to make use of podcasts, audiobooks, and media remote control, and also how to set up Bluetooth devices and audio routes.

Chapter 8: Productivity and Organization

In this chapter, you will learn how to enhance your productivity. You will learn how to sync calendars to make use of reminders and capture ideas with the use of notes and voice dictation. You will also learn how to make the best use of Find My App for people and devices.

Chapter 9: Advanced Customization and Settings

In this chapter, you will learn more about the various settings that can be of immense contribution and benefit to your use of the watch. You will learn about the various accessibility features, customization of your sound and display, privacy and security essentials, and also you will learn about the use of the control center.

Chapter 10: Troubleshooting and Maintenance

In this chapter, you will learn about the various problems that may arise when you are using your watch, and you will also get to know how to fix these problems when they arise. You will also learn how to reset and restore your watch.

Chapter 11: Unlocking Hidden Potentials

There is so much more to your Apple Watch Series 9 than you know and that is what this chapter will reveal. Here you will learn about the amazing things you can do with your Apple Watch series 9 like having it control your home and lots more. Having read the overview; get set to dive into the real deal. This book has been written with illustrations to help you out with technical areas. Ensure you have your watch close by as you read this book so you get to practice what you are reading in real-time!

CHAPTER 1
UNBOXING AND INITIAL SETUP

When you work so hard for your money to buy your Apple Watch, you will be left grabbing a lovely, long, and slender box. Colors, however, may be quite different as this is based on your preference.

The box contains the following;

- **Apple Watch**: Ensure you keep all of the packaging until you are very sure you will have no need to return the Apple Watch for any reason. Note however that the standard return period for Apple is 14 days and this is for products that are purchased directly from them. If you happen to buy your Apple Watch from a third party, ensure you check with them for their own return policies.
- **Documentation**: Usually, the documentation includes a small pamphlet, a sheet of Apple logo stickers, and some more bits of information.
- **USB-C charging cable**: You are to make use of this cable in connecting the Apple Watch to your computer or USB power adapter for charging.

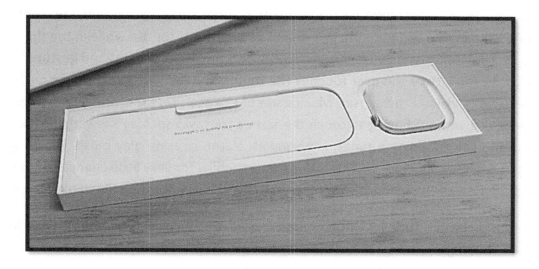

In the second box are your watch bands. Ensure you are on the lookout for the bot on one end of the box which is an indication for you to pull it open.

Unveiling Your Apple Watch Series 9

Apple unveiled the Apple Watch Series 9 which features quite an improved performance due to the S9 Apple silicon chip, a "Double Tap" hand gesture used for the interaction with the device without the use of touch, precision finding for iPhone, and lots more. The Series 9 has been redesigned in an amazing way which also includes the inclusion of a new Apple silicon chip. It has about 60% more transistors and is 30% faster than the S8 chip. Furthermore, embedded in it are four-core neural engines for 2x faster neural tasks. Requests from Siri can now be processed on the Apple Watch, ensuring that it is faster and more secure, and the voice assistant can also gain access to health data for the first time. Dictation on the Series 9 is also about 25% more accurate than the Series 8 and this is due to secure on-device processing. It keeps the same 18-hour all-day battery life.

For the first time, the Apple Watch Series 9 can employ Precision Finding for an iPhone, just as the iPhone can with an AirTag, thanks to Ultra-Wideband support. It is also more closely linked to the HomePod. When an Apple Watch Series 9 user comes within four meters of a HomePod that is playing audio, Now Playing will instantly launch to control the media. If HomePod is not playing anything, media suggestions will show at the top of the Smart Stack. Also, the Series 9 has a much brighter always-on Retina display that can now go up to about 2000 nits, which is two times the brightness of the Apple Watch Series. It can also be limited to just one of its brightness for use while in the theater or at night. The Apple Series 9 can be controlled with the use of a new hand gesture known as "Double Tap". Here the user touches the thumb and index finger together such as with the use of a Vision Pro headset. Making use of this gesture, users are able to interact with the device without having to touch the screen for tasks such as answering or putting an end to a call, stopping a timer, snoozing an alarm, pausing play music, bringing up the Smart Stack, and lots more. This is done by searching for very little changes to movement and the flow of the blood with the use of the accelerometer and blood oxygen sensor.

The Apple Watch Series 9 can be found in a new Pink color option. It also has Starlight, Silver, Midnight, and PRODUCT (RED). The stainless-steel version can be found in the colors Silver, Gold, and Graphite. The Apple Watch Series 9 is created with more recycled materials and comes in a smaller, and more environmentally friendly box. A redesigned Sport Loop band also contains 82% recycled yarn. Leather will no longer be available on new Apple Watch bands, but the company will offer a variety of new "FineWoven" bands, as well as bands from Hermès and Nike. The Apple Watch Series 9 is the successor to the Series 8, which introduced body temperature sensors and cycle tracking, as well as a more robust gyroscope and high dynamic range accelerometer and Crash Detection.

Charging and Power Management

Just like your normal phone that needs juice, your Apple Watch also needs to be charged. There is also a need for you to know how best to manage the power options on the watch so you can get to use it for a longer period of time before it runs out of juice. In this section, you will learn about how to charge and manage the power options on your watch.

Setting up the charger

- Ensure you are in a well-ventilated area then place your charger or charging cable on a flat surface. Usually, your Apple Watch ought to come with the Apple Watch Magnetic Fast Charger to USB-C Cable or you can also choose to make use of the Apple Watch Magnetic Charging Cable. Also, you can choose to make use of a MagSafe Duo Charger or Apple Watch Magnetic Charging Dock (usually sold separately).
- Plug **the charging cable into the power adapter** (it's also sold separately).
- Plug **the adapter into a power outlet.**

Note however that fast charging needs an 18W or greater USB-C Power Adapter. Also, be aware that fast charging is not available in all regions. The rear of your Apple Watch should be connected to the Apple Watch Magnetic Charging Cable or Apple Watch Magnetic Fast Charger to USB-C cable. Your Apple Watch is properly positioned by the charging cable's concave end, which magnetically attaches to the device's back. If your watch is not in silent mode, the Apple Watch will chime when charging starts and display a charging icon on the watch face. When the Apple Watch is running low on battery, the sign is red; when it is charging, it is green. Yellow is the color of the charging icon while Apple Watch is in Low Power Mode. You are at liberty to charge your Apple Watch in a flat position with its band wide open or on its side.

- If you are making use of the Apple Watch Magnetic Charging Dock or MagSafe Duo Charger: Ensure your **Apple Watch is laid on the dock.**

- If your battery happens to be very low: There may be the presence of an image of the Apple Watch Magnetic Fast Charger to USB-C Cable or Apple Watch Magnetic Charging Cable and the low battery sign on the screen.

If you would like to see the power left on your watch, tap the side button to open the Control Center. To get this done at a faster pace, you can customize the watch face by adding a battery complication to the watch face.

Save Power

Enabling Low Power Mode will prolong the life of your battery. By doing this, you can turn off the Always On Display, background blood oxygen and heart rate monitoring, and heart rate notifications. Emergency warnings might not be received, other notifications might be delayed, and some cellular and Wi-Fi connections might be restricted. Cellular is disabled until you need it, such as when you send a message or stream music. It is worth noting that Low Power Mode will be switched off when the battery is charged up to about 80%.

- Tap **the side button** to get the Control Center opened.
- Touch **the battery percentage**, then switch **on Low Power Mode**.
- If you would like to confirm your choice, navigate **downwards, then touch Turn On**.

You can choose to switch on for, then pick On for 1 Day, On for 2 Days, or On for 3 Days. If you have your battery-powered devices like AirPods connected to your Apple Watch via Bluetooth, touch the battery percentage in the Control Center, then switch the Digital Crown to get a view of the charge left for your headphones.

youtube

When the level of the battery goes down to about 10 percent or much lower, you will be alerted by your battery and it will also provide you with the opportunity to enter Low Power Mode. **If you would like to go back to normal power mode;**

- Tap **the side button** to open the Control Center.
- Touch **the battery percentage**, then switch off the **Low Power Mode**.

You are also able to check the time you last charged;

- Open the **Settings application** on your Apple Watch.
- **Touch Battery.** The Battery screen will display the battery percentage left, and a graph that shows the details of the recent history of the battery charge will be made bare while also showing the information about when the battery was last charged.

Battery Health

You can find out the capacity of your Apple Watch battery in relation to when you just bought it. Follow the settings below to get this done;

- Open the **Settings application** on your Apple Watch.
- Touch **Battery and then tap Battery Health**.

If you would like to bring a reduction to battery aging, the Apple Watch makes use of on-device machine learning to learn about daily charging routines so it can wait to get charged past 80 percent while there is a need for you to make use of it.

- Open the **Settings application** on your Apple Watch.
- Touch Battery, then pick **Battery Health**.
- Switch on **Optimized Battery Charging**.

Tips to preserve your battery life

There are a few ways by which you can preserve battery life on your Apple Watch;

- Power Saving Mode should be activated to switch off the heart rate sensor while exercising while jogging or walking. Launch the Apple Watch app on your iPhone, select **My Watch > Workout,** and enable Power Saving Mode. It should be noted that calorie burn estimates might not be as precise if the heart rate sensor is turned off.
- The built-in heart rate sensor can be substituted with a Bluetooth chest strap for longer workouts. Make sure the Bluetooth chest strap is in pairing mode, then go to Settings on your Apple Watch, select Bluetooth, and pick a health device from the list.

- If you are quite active with the use of your hands and your watch display turns on more than you think it ought to, you can prevent the display from switching on each time you lift up your wrist. Open **Settings** on Apple Watch, choose **General**, choose **Wake Screen**, and turn **Wake Screen on Wrist Raise off**. Whenever you have a need to switch on the display, all you have to do is touch it or press **the Digital Crown**.
- Disabling Bluetooth on your iPhone increases the battery drain on your Apple Watch. For much more power-efficient communication between the devices. Ensure you keep Bluetooth enabled on your iPhone.

Low Power Mode, which was introduced with watchOS 9, is a simple way to increase the battery life of your Apple Watch when necessary, such as if you're on a lengthy flight or are without a charger for the evening. Turn it on by navigating to Settings > Battery or by sliding up to Control Center and tapping on the battery percentage. By disabling background sensor readings such as heart rate measurements, high and low heart rate notifications, irregular rhythm notifications, and blood oxygen measurements, Low Power Mode increases battery life by turning off the always-on display, limiting the Apple Watch's cellular and Wi-Fi connections, and turning off the always-on display. Your Apple Watch will make an effort to retrieve alerts about once every hour when it is not linked to your iPhone. Low Power Mode automatically ends when the Apple Watch battery is 80% charged.

Pairing with Your iPhone

To use your Apple Watch, there is a need for you to ensure it is paired with your iPhone. Configure assistants on your iPhone and Apple Watch in order to help you pair and set up your watch. To ensure this pairing is successful, ensure you are making use of an iPhone Xs or; later with iOs17 or later

Before you commence the pairing, ensure you do the following;

- Update your iPhone to the latest version of iOS. Open the **Settings application** on your iPhone, touch **General,** and then **touch Software Update.**
- Ensure that the Bluetooth of your iPhone is switched on, and it is connected to Wi-Fi or a cellular network. To check for this, swipe **down from the top-right**

corner of the screen of the iPhone to display **the Control Center.** The Bluetooth and Wi-Fi buttons should also be switched on.

Once the above has been completed, follow the steps below to commence the pairing;

Step 1: Turn on and pair your Apple Watch

- Place your **Apple Watch on your wrist.** Modify the band or pick a band size to ensure that your Watch fits well and is also comfortable on your wrist.
- To switch on your Apple Watch, touch **and hold the side button** until you are able to see the Apple logo.

  If for any reason your Apple Watch doesn't come on, there may be a need for you to change your battery.
- Hold your **iPhone close to your Apple Watch**, pause for the Apple Watch pairing screen to be displayed on your iPhone, and then touch **Continue**. You can also open the Apple Watch application on your iPhone, and then touch **Pair New Watch.**
- Touch **Set Up for Myself.**

- Whenever you are prompted, place your **iPhone so that your Apple Watch will be displayed in the viewfinder in the Apple Watch app**. This will then ensure the two devices are paired.

Step 2: Set up your Apple Watch

- If this is your first Apple Watch, touch **Set Up Apple Watch**, then go after the instructions on your iPhone and Apple Watch to complete the setup. If you have configured another Apple Watch with the use of your current iPhone, a screen will show that says **Make This Your New Apple Watch**. Touch **Apps & Data** and **Settings** to see just how Express Setup will help with the configuration of your new watch. The touch continues. If you would like to choose how your new watch is configured, touch **Customize Setting**s. Then choose a backup from another previous Apple Watch to restore. You can also choose to touch **Set Up as New Apple Watch** if there is a need for you to totally personalize the settings of your new device.

- **Follow the instructions on your screen to configure the following;**

  o Insert your **Apple ID and password.**
  o Creat**e a passcode**; either a standard four-digit passcode or a long passcode, which will have a need for six digits.

○ Personalize configurations for text size, as an optional insert personal information like date of birth and height that are utilized for the purpose of fitness and health, and pick the health notifications you would like to receive. These settings can be altered after you have configured your Apple Watch.

Step 3: Activate cellular device

If you have an Apple Watch with cellular, you can activate cellular service while setup is ongoing. If you would not like to, you are able to activate it much later in the Apple Watch app on your iPhone. Your iPhone and Apple Watch have to make use of the same cellular carrier. Nevertheless, if you configure an Apple Watch for someone in your Family Sharing group, that watch can make use of a cellular carrier that is quite different from the one used on the iPhone you manage it with. It is worth noting that cellular service is not available in every region.

Step 4: Keep your devices close as they sync

When pairing is complete and the watch is ready to use, the watch face appears on your Apple Watch. While your Apple Watch is synchronizing, tap **Get to Know Your Watch** to discover more about it. On your iPhone, you may read this user manual, view Apple Watch tips, and find out what's new. You may get this information by launching the Apple Watch app on your iPhone when your Apple Watch is configured, and then tapping Discover.

Below are some troubleshooting pairings that can be of great help to you;

- **If you happen to see a watch face when you are attempting to pair:** Your Apple Watch has already been paired with an iPhone. There is then a need for you to first erase all Apple Watch content and then have the settings reset.
- **If the camera doesn't start the process of pairing**: Touch **Pair Apple Watch** Manually at the lower part of the iPhone screen then follow the instructions on the screen.

Setting up more than one Apple Watch

It is quite amazing that you can pair your iPhone with more than just one watch. In this section, you will learn about how you can set up more than just one Apple Watch. You can get this done the very same way you did the first one. All you have to do is bring your iPhone close to your Apple Watch, pause for the Apple Watch pairing screen to be **displayed on your iPhone then proceed to touch Pair or you can choose to follow the steps below;**

- Open the **Apple Watch app on your iPhone**.
- Touch **My Watch**, then touch **All Watches at the upper part of the screen**.
- Touch **Add Watch** and then follow the instructions on the screen.

Switching to another Apple Watch

Your iPhone immediately establishes a connection with the linked Apple Watch you are wearing after detecting it. If you would like to switch, simply switch to another Apple Watch and lift your wrist. **Note however that you are also able to complete this switch process manually by following the steps below;**

- Open the **Apple Watch app on your iPhone.**
- Touch **My Watch**, then choose **All Watches at the upper part of your screen.**
- Switch off **Auto Switch** then proceed to make a choice of another watch.

If you would like to see and be sure that your Apple Watch is connected to your iPhone, tap the side button in order to open the Control Center, then search for the connected status icon.

Pair Your Apple Watch with a new iPhone

Change is the only constant thing hence this section will explain the steps you need to take to pair your new iPhone with your watch. Follow the steps below to learn more about this.

- Make use of the iCloud Backup to back up the iPhone currently paired with your Apple Watch.

- Configure your new iPhone. On the Apps & Data screen, pick **the option of restoring from an iCloud backup,** then choose the **latest backup.**
- Proceed **with iPhone setup** and, whenever there is a prompt, make the choice of using your Apple Watch with your new iPhone.

Whenever the iPhone setup is complete, your Apple Watch will then prompt you to pair it with a new iPhone. Touch OK on your Apple Watch, then insert its passcode. When you have a need to switch to a new application, the application you were making use of will not remain open or use up system resources, but there may still be a need for a refresh; check for updates and new content in the background. Refreshing applications in the **background can make use of power. If you would like to maximize battery life, you are able to switch off this option.**

- Open the **Settings application** on your Apple Watch.
- Navigate to **General > Background Application Refresh**.
- Switch off **Background App Refresh** in order to prevent all applications from refreshing. You can also choose to scroll down, and then switch refresh off for individual applications.

Setting Up Cellular and Family Setup

You can make calls, reply to messages, use Walkie-Talkies, stream music and podcasts, and get notifications, and more with an Apple Watch with cellular and a cellular connection to the same carrier as your iPhone— all without your iPhone or a Wi-Fi connection.

Note: Not all carriers or locations offer cellular service.

Add Apple Watch to your cellular plan

You can activate cellular service on your Apple Watch by following the set of instructions while you are setting up your Apple Watch after unboxing.

- Open the **Apple Watch app on your iPhone**.
- Touc**h My Watch, then touch Cellular.**

Transferring an existing cellular plan to a new Apple Watch

You can send an existing cellular plan from your Apple Watch with the use of cellular to another Apple Watch with cellular by making use of the set of instructions below;

- While wearing your Apple Watch, open the **Apple Watch app on your iPhone.**
- Touch **My Watch, touch Cellular,** and then touch **the icon close to your cellular plan.**
- Touch **Remove (name of carrier) plan,** then make a confirmation of your choice. There may be a need for you to contact your carrier to take off the Apple Watch from your cellular plan.
- Remove your old watch, wear your other Apple Watch with cellular, touch **My Watch, and then choose Cellular.**

Switch Cellular either on or off

When an iPhone is nearby, a Wi-Fi network you've already connected to on your iPhone, or a cellular connection is available, your Apple Watch with cellular makes use of the strongest available network connection. You can disable cellular service to conserve battery life, for instance. Just carry out these actions.

- Tap **the side button to launch the Control Center.**
- Tap the **network icon, then switch Cellular either off or on.**

The Cellular button becomes green when your Apple Watch has a cellular connection and your iPhone is not close by. It is worth noting that switching on cellular for a long period of time makes use of more battery power. Furthermore, there are some applications that may not update if there is no connection to your iPhone.

Check Cellular signal strength

Try one of the following when connected to a cellular network;

- Make **use of the Explorer watch face,** which makes use of green dots to display cellular signal strength. Four dots mean a good connection. One dot is a poor connection.
- Open **Control Center.** The green bars at the upper part display the cellular connection status.

Check cellular data usage

- Open the **Settings application on your Apple Watch.**

- Touch **Cellular**, then move down to have a view of the amount of data you have used while in the current period.

Family Setup

You can choose to configure and manage the Apple Watch for a person who doesn't have their own iPhone- your school-aged child or parent, for instance. To get this done, there is a need for you to be the family organizer or parent/guardian in your Family Sharing group. The iPhone you make use of in initially pairing and then configuring the Apple Watch must be within normal Bluetooth range which is about 33 feet or 10 meters of the Apple Watch to manage the configurations and update the software. The person you get to set up Apple Watch for must be a part of your Family Sharing group and also must have a cellular-capable Apple Watch.

With the use of the Apple Watch app and Screen Time on your iPhone, you can effectively manage the following;

- Communication limits and safety.
- A schedule for time away from the screen.
- School time; which helps to limit a feature that helps to limit some Apple Watch features while school is on.
- Mail and Calendar configurations for iCloud, Gmail, and other services.
- Restriction configurations for explicit content, purchases, and privacy.

Some of the interactions between a family member's Apple Watch and the iPhone that was used to set it up are restricted. For instance, you cannot transfer tasks from the managed Apple Watch to the iPhone or unlock a paired iPhone from an Apple Watch you set up for a family member. When you uninstall an app from a family member's Apple Watch, the iPhone that was used to set it up doesn't get the same treatment.

Set up your family member's Apple Watch

Configuring an Apple Watch for a family member is just like configuring a watch for yourself. Before you establish a pair and configure a watch for your family member, erase the watch so that you are absolutely sure that it has no content whatsoever in it.

- Have your family members wear their Apple Watch. Modify the band or pick a band size so that the Apple Watch fits totally and comfortably on their wrist.
- To switch on the Apple Watch, touch and hold **the side button** until you can no longer see the Apple logo.
- Drag **your iPhone close to the Apple Watch**, pause for the Apple Watch pairing screen to be displayed on your iPhone, and then choose **Continue.**
- Touch **Set Up for a Family Member, t**hen touch **Continue** on the following screen.
- Whenever there is a prompt, place your iPhone so that the Apple Watch shows in the viewfinder in the Apple Watch app. This will then pair both devices.
- Touch **Set up Apple Watch and follow the instructions on your iPhone and Apple Watch to complete the setup.**

Manage a Family Member Apple Watch

- Open **the Apple Watch app** on the iPhone used in managing the watch.
- Touch **My Watch**, touch **Family Watches,** touch a watch then choose **Done.**

Set up Screen Time

To set up controls for a family member's Apple Watch, use Screen Time. You can limit the contacts and apps your family members can use to contact those connections with the help of Screen Time, which also allows you to schedule time away from the screen. You can set restrictions on explicit content, location data, and app and iTunes Store purchases.

Follow the steps below to have your screen set up;

- Open the **Apple Watch application** on the iPhone used for the management of the watch.
- Touc**h My Watch, touch Family Watches, touch a watch, and then choose Done.**
- Touch **Screen Time**, touch **Screen Time Settings**, and then touch **Turn on Screen Time**.
- On the screen that follows, set options for allowable content, communication safety, time away from screens, and applications and website limits.
- Design a **Screen Time passcode.**

School Time on Apple Watch

Parents and guardians can remotely activate Do Not Disturb on children's watches and display a special watch face with minimum input thanks to a Family Setup feature called "Schooltime." On your personal Apple Watch, you can use Schooltime whenever you need to concentrate on something, even if you are not interested in Family Setup. When you want to silence alerts and block apps but still want to be able to simply see the time without visual distractions, you can use Schooltime as an alternative to Do Not Disturb or Theater Mode. It helps remove distractions from your Apple Watch. Additionally, if Schooltime is activated, you won't have to worry about missing any Emergency Calls because you will still get them.

Follow the steps below to Set up Schooltime;

- Open t**he Apple Watch application** on the iPhone used for the management of the watch.
- Touch **My Watch, touch Family Watches, and then touch a watch.**
- Touch **Done, then choose Schooltime.**
- Switch on **Schooltime, then touch Edit Schedule.**
- Make a choice of the days and times you would like to have Schooltime active on the watch.
- Touch **Add time** if you would like to configure various schedules during a day from 0.00 a.m. to noon and then 1:00 p.m. to 3:00 p.m. for instance.

To Exit Schooltime

Your family member may have a need to leave Schooltime temporarily; maybe to check activity rings.

- All you need to do is touch the display, touch and hold **the Digital Crown**, and then touch **Exit.**

If for any reason you happen to exit Schooltime during scheduled hours, the Schooltime watch face goes back when you bring down your wrist. During non-scheduled hours, Schooltime will be inactive until the following start time, or until you touch the Schooltime icon in the Control Center.

See when Schooltime was unlocked

Anytime any of your family members leave Scholtime, you will get a report that informs you about the time they left and for how long they left. Follow the steps below to be able to see the report;

- Open the **Apple Watch application** on the iPhone that is used for the management of the watch.
- Touch **My Watch, touch Family Watches, and then touch a watch.**
- Touch **Done,** then touch **Schooltime** to view reports for the days, times, and durations Schooltime was unlocked.

The report will also be displayed on the Apple Watch. If you would like to see it, open the Settings application on the Apple Watch, then choose Schooltime. Your family member can activate Schooltime while it isn't in use, for example, if they have joined an after-school study club that takes place outside of the allotted time and don't want to be disturbed. All you have to do is tap the side button, then touch the Schooltime icon in the Control Center. To leave Schooltime, tap and touch the Digital Crown, then touch Exit. Schooltime will be switched on once more when it has been scheduled or when it is switched on in the Control Center.

Playing music on a managed Apple Watch

You can listen to Apple Music on your managed Apple Watch if you're a member of a Family Sharing group that has a family membership to the service and you have a Wi-Fi or cellular connection.

- Open the Music app on your managed Apple Watch to navigate to the Listen Now screen, where you see music chosen for you depending on your listening habits. You are also able to scroll down and touch a playlist designed for kids and teenagers by editors of Apple Music.

If you would like to play music from the library, touch the play icon, and then do any of the following;

- Touch **Radio** to get to listen to Apple Music Radio and genre stations.

- Touch **Library** to search music stored on Apple Watch.
- Touch **Search,** then type dictates, or you can also choose to **subscribe to an artist, album, or playlist.**

- Make use of the music controls in the Music application and Now Playing application in order to choose and also play music. If you would like to learn how to include and take off music on your Apple Watch, check out Add Music and Remove Music.

Add and play podcasts on a managed Apple Watch

You can choose to follow and stream podcasts directly on a managed Apple Watch.

Play podcasts

Open the Podcasts application on your managed Apple Watch, then do any of the following:

- In the Listen Now screen, touch a podcast you are following.
- Say anything like "Siri, play the podcast A Beloved Wife". Your Apple Watch will then play the latest episode of the podcast.
- Touch the **play button**, touch **Library**, and then touch a **show you usually follow.**
- Touch the **play button**, touch **Search,** insert the **name of a podcast,** then touch **the show.**

If you would like to follow the show, touch Follow. Touch **your preferred episode to play it.**

See activity and health reports for family members

With the permission of your family members, you can see reports of their activity and also their health information.

See health information

If your family member has given room for you to view their health information, you can see more information about their activity and also information about time in daylight, hearing, and heart rate information.

- Open **the Health application on your iPhone, then touch Sharing.**
- Touch **the name of your family member beneath Sharing with You.**
- Touch **Health Categories**, then touch **your preferred category.**

Add health details and Medical ID

Follow these steps to insert your family member's health details or Medical ID:

- Open the **Apple Watch app** on the iPhone which is used for the management of the watch.
- Touch **My Watch, touch Family Watches, and touch your preferred watch.**
- Touch **Done**, touch **Health**, then touch **Request (family member's name) Health Data.**
- Touch **Request Health Data**, and then a notification will be sent to the managed watch. After your family member has made a choice to share their health data, get the following done;
  - Touch Health Details to insert information like birthdate, height, and weight.
  - Touch Set up Medical ID to include emergency contacts and more.

If your family member decides to share this information from their health application with you, you will be able to see health details and Medical ID on the iPhone used for the management of the Apple Watch and on the watch.

Monitor time in daylight for Family members

The ambient light sensor in Apple Watch SE (2nd generation) and Apple Watch Series 6 and later models assess how much time each family member spends outdoors during the day.

Review a family member's time in daylight data

If your family member happens to be sharing their health information with you, you can monitor their details in the Health app on the iPhone.

- Open the **Health app on your iPhone, then touch Sharing.**
- Touch **the name of your family member beneath Sharing With You.**

- Touch **Health Categories**, touch **Other Data**, and then touch **Time in Daylight.**

Switch off time in daylight

- Open the **Settings application on the managed Apple Watch.**
- Navigate to **Privacy & Security > Health.**
- Touch **Time in Daylight, then switch off Time in Daylight**

You can also use the Apple Watch management software on your iPhone, select **My Watch, and then select Family Watches.** Turn off **Time in Daylight after selecting Done and Privacy.**

Use Apple Cash Family on a family member's Apple Watch

In order for the kids and teenagers in your family sharing group to use their Apple Watch to make purchases and give and receive money in Messages, you, as the group administrator, must set up Apple Cash. You can even restrict the recipients of your child's money transfers, receive alerts when your child makes transactions, and lock their account. It is worth noting that Apple Cash Family is not available in all regions and is only supported on iPhone SE and iPhone 6 and later versions.

Set up Apple Cash Family

If you would like to configure Apple Cash Family, there is a need for you to be the family organizer, and the members of the family you want to set up Apple Cash for must be below 18 years of age.

- On your **iPhone, locate Settings> your name > Family Sharing.**
- Pick **a child or teenager, then touch Apple Cash.**
- Touch **Set up Apple Cash**, then follow the onscreen instructions to configure their account. It is worth noting that in the U.S., your family member is able to send, receive, and also ask for money and make use of Apple Pay for their purchases.

Manage Apple Cash on a family member's Apple Watch

- Launch **the Wallet application** on the iPhone used for the management of the watch.
- Touch **your Apple Cash card.**

- Touch **a name underneath the family.**
- **Configure the following options in accordance with your preference;**
  - Make a choice of the person your family member can send money to.
  - Choose to get a notification when your family member completes a transaction.
- Touch **Send Money** to launch the **Messages application and send money with the use of Apple Pay.**

Touch Lock Apple Cash to prevent the family member from completing payments with the use of Apple Pay or sending and receiving money in the Messages application. Tap Transactions on this page, open the Wallet app on your iPhone, and then tap your Apple Cash card to view a family member's transactions. When you touch Transactions in [year], the transactions for your family members are displayed underneath Latest Transactions.

Touring Watch Faces and Customization

Customize your Apple Watch face so that it will appear just the way you want it to and will also offer the functions you are in need of. Make a choice of your design, modify colors and features, and then include it in your collections. Change faces at any time to have a view of the right timekeeping tools or to have things shaken up. The Face Gallery in the Apple Watch is the easiest way to catch a glimpse of all the watch faces available to you. Personalize one of them, and include it in your collection. If your iPhone is not handy, you can choose to have its face personalized with the use of your watch.

Face Gallery

The simplest way to view every watch face that is offered is through the Face Gallery in the Apple Watch app. You may edit it, select complexities, and then add the face to your collection whenever you find one that looks intriguing—all from the gallery. Launch the Apple Watch application on your iPhone, then touch Face Gallery at the lower part of the screen. In the Face Gallery, touch a face, then touch a feature like color or style. As you experiment with diverse options, the face at the top will keep changing so you can be sure that the design is just perfect for you.

To add a face,

- Navigate to the face gallery, choose **your preferred face, and then make a choice of the features and complications you want.**
- Touch **Add**. The face will then be added to your collection and it will then become the current face on your Apple Watch.

Activity

1. Configure the power management settings on your watch and charge it.
2. Configure Cellular and Family Setup.
3. Pair your watch with your iPhone.
4. Check out the various watch faces and customize the exact one you would like to use.

CHAPTER 2
NAVIGATING YOUR APPLE WATCH

Now that you have unboxed your amazing watch and configured the necessary settings with the use of the settings application, it is time to experiment and check out all you can do with your Apple Watch Series 9. To be able to do this, navigation is a key aspect and you need to learn how to properly roam around your Apple Watch. In this chapter, you will learn all you need to know and lots more, it's quite a loaded chapter!

Mastering the Hardware Components

In this section, you will learn about the major hardware components in the Apple Watch 9 series and how best you can make use of them;

- **Side button**: Switch your Apple Watch either on or off, display or conceal the dock, make use of Apple Pay, or employ the use of the SOS feature.
- **Digital Crown**: Open Siri, click twice to go back to the former application, navigate upwards or downwards the list, zoom in and out, and lots more.
- **Display**: here you get to see the cool stuff shown in the windows on your Apple Watch.
- **Electrical heart sensor**: Take a measurement of the electrical signals in your blood, enabling your watch to do an ECG and give you accurate heart health diagnostics.
- **Optical heart sensor**: this helps you to measure how fast your heart beats and the rate at which your blood flows. Although it is not as accurate as an electrical heart sensor for certain measurements, the optical heart sensor can be quite handy while a workout is ongoing.
- **Blood oxygen sensor**: with this component, you are able to measure the saturation of the oxygen in your blood. Making use of clusters of red, green, and infrared lights, the sensor helps with the detection of the color of the blood flowing through your veins in order to determine the amount of oxygen it has.
- **Speaker/air vents**: with this, you can hear audio output and also equalize the pressure to aid the altimeter in offering more accurate altitude measurements.
- **Band release buttons:** Tap this to let go of the bands that are connected to your Apple Watch, and then slide the bans out to get them removed.

- **Action button (Ultra Only)**: enables swift and easy access to an application or feature you make use of often and need to swiftly return to often, without having to check the Apple Watch applications on your display.
- **Microphone**: For instructions or content delivery, speak into your Apple Watch. Making phone conversations, dictating text messages, and using other apps that accept audio input, such as the Siri built-in assistant, are all made possible by this function.

The Digital Crown: Navigation Hub

When users rotate the Digital Crown, data is generated that you may utilize to improve or simplify user interactions with your app, such as scrolling or using built-in or custom controls. With watchOS 10, the Digital Crown assumes a more important position as the main input for navigation. The Digital Crown may be used to scroll vertically between the apps on the Home Screen or to view widgets in the Smart Stack on the watch face. Turning the Digital Crown within an app allows users to browse among list views and pages of varying heights as well as move between tabs that are vertically paginated. In addition to being used for navigation, using the Digital Crown also creates data that can be used to improve or simplify interactions with your app, such as viewing data or using pre-built or custom controls. Most Apple Watch models offer haptic feedback for the Digital Crown which provides people with quite a more tactile experience as they navigate through content. By default, the system offers linear haptic detents or taps as people switch the Digital Crown a certain distance. Specific system controls such as table view, provide detents as new items scroll onto the screen.

Anchor your application's navigation to the Digital Crown

Starting with watchOS10, turning the Digital Crown is the most important way people move within various applications in the watch. List, tab, and scroll views are oriented in a vertical manner, enabling people to make use of the Digital Crown to move with ease between the important elements of the interface of your application. Whenever you are anchoring interactions to the Digital Crown, ensure you back them up with corresponding touchscreen interactions.

Consider using the Digital Crown to inspect data in contexts where navigation isn't important

In contexts where the Digital Crown has no need to move through lists or between various pages, it is a very important tool to inspect data in your application. For instance, the World Clock, when the Digital Crown is turned, helps to advance the time of day at a chosen location, enabling people to compare diverse times of the day to their current time.

Provide visual feedback in response to Digital Crown interactions

For instance, pickers alter the currently shown value as people make use of the Digital Crown. If you track turns in a direct manner, make use of this data to update your interface in a programmatic manner. If you fail to offer visual feedback, people are most likely to assume that turning the Digital Crown has no effect on your application.

Update your interface to match the speed with which people turn the Digital Crown

It works effectively to use this speed to decide how quickly changes are made since people anticipate the Digital Crown to give them exact control over an interface. Stay away from updating stuff at a pace that makes choosing values challenging.

Use the default haptic feedback when it makes sense in your application

Turn off the detents if the haptic feedback doesn't feel natural in your app's environment, such as when the animation doesn't match the default detents. Additionally, tables' haptic feedback behavior can be changed such that linear detents are used in place of row-based detents. For instance, linear detents might provide users with a more uniform experience if your table has rows that are noticeably diverse in height. **For simplicity's sake, below are some of the things you can do with the use of the Digital Crown;**

- **Open an app**: with your app gallery open, zoom in by **spinning your Digital Crown** to open any app you have centered on the screen.

- **Reopen a previous app**: Tap **the Digital Crown two times** to go back to the app you were using before.
- **Control Volume**: If you are streaming Spotify or listening to a podcast, open Now Playing on your device and make use of the Digital Crown to increase or reduce the volume. This works well for music, podcasts, audiobooks, and any other thing you are streaming or have saved on your device.
- **Skim content:** You can spin the Digital Crown within almost all applications to navigate through content. Furthermore, you can also make use of this same functionality to navigate through menus, which includes those of the watch itself.
- **Get a better look**: In your navigation application, spin **the Digital Crown** to either zoom in or out on your route or points of interest.

Side Button Magic: Functions and Shortcuts

The side button is an important feature in the Apple Watch Series 9 and it has so many functions some of which will be discussed in this section.

Emergency SOS

When you place a call using Emergency SOS, your Apple Watch immediately contacts the nearest emergency services and provides them with your location. If you don't opt out, your Apple Watch texts your current position to your emergency contacts after the call ends. After you activate SOS mode, your emergency contacts will receive notifications when your location changes for a while. An Apple Watch or adjacent iPhone must have a cellular connection or be connected to Wi-Fi calling and the Internet for Emergency SOS to work. You might have to pick the emergency assistance you require in various nations and regions. You can select police, fire, or ambulance on the Chinese mainland, for instance.

To make use of this service simply get the following done;

- Tap and hold **the side button** of your watch until the Emergency Call slider displays.
- Move the Emergency Call slider to commence the call instantly. Or you can continue to hold **the side button**; after a countdown, your watch calls emergency services instantly.

Furthermore, with the use of your Apple Watch Series 9, you will be able to call emergency service and also send a message to any of your emergency contacts when a severe car crash is detected. **You can alter your settings so that having to hold the side button will not call emergency services instantly;**

- Open the **Apple Watch application on your iPhone,** then touch the **My Watch tab**.
- Touch **Emergency SOS**.
- Switch off the **Hold Side Button to Dial.**

If you commenced the Emergency SOS countdown mistakenly, all you have to do is let go of the side button. If the call has been placed already but you have no need for emergency services, don't hang up. Wait a little until some answers then explain that you do not need help. Once that has been done, your watch will then ask if there is still a need to send a text message to your emergency contacts. Touch No if you would like to have the text canceled. Your Apple Watch will notify you four hours after your emergency call that your location is being shared with your emergency contacts. To stop sharing your location, choose Stop Sharing in the notification.

Making Purchases with Apple Pay

With the use of your Apple Watch Series 9, you can make use of Apple Pay in stores, restaurants, gas stations, taxis, or anywhere you see the Apple Pay symbol.

To make payment with the use of your Apple Watch, follow the steps below;

- Tap **the side button twice**.
- Your default card will then open up instantly. Move down to make a choice of another card.
- Hold the **display of your Apple Watch** close to the contactless reader until you have a feeling of a gentle tap and you also hear a beep sound.

Embracing Assistive Touch Gestures

AssistiveTouch is activated when a blue ring appears around the Apple Watch screen when your wrist is raised. Clench your fist twice fast to start AssistiveTouch. This visual cue's color can be modified by going to

Accessibility

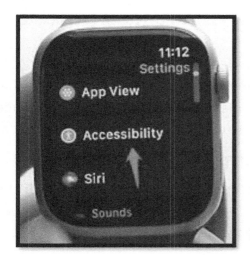

AssistiveTouch

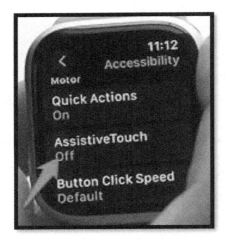

> Color. Alternatively, you can disable the visual signal by selecting Activation Gesture under **Accessibility > AssistiveTouch > Hand Gestures**. Once you have activated AssistiveTouch, a focus ring will be displayed around the first item on your screen. The focus ring shows that you can touch the item with the use of AssistiveTouch.

With the use of default actions, you can choose to navigate your Apple Watch Series 9 with the use of these hand gestures:

- **Move to the next item:** Pinch **(Touch your pointer finger to your thumb).**
- **Move back one item:** Pinch **twice (Touch your pointer finger to your thumb two times swiftly).**
- **Touch an item:** **Clench (close your hand into a fist)**
- **Bring up the action menu:** Clench twice (close your hand into a fist two times swiftly). The action menu will allow you to perform some actions with the use of AssistiveTouch like scrolling, tapping the Digital Crown, and lots more.

Customizing Assistive Touch hand gestures

- Launch the **Settings application** on your Apple Watch or the Apple Watch on your iPhone.
- Touch **Accessibility > Assistive Touch > Hand Gestures**.

- Touch **a preferred gesture,** then choose the action that you would like to perform when you make that gesture.

You can also choose to customize the hand gesture that helps with the activation of the AssistiveTouch. Navigate to the **Accessibility > Assistive Touch > Hand Gestures > Activation Gestures.**

Use Manual Scanning or Auto-Scanning

When Manual Scanning is enabled in **Settings > Accessibility > AssistiveTouch > Scanning Style**, you can use hand movements to control when AssistiveTouch goes to the next item on the screen and when an item is pressed. Your Apple Watch will automatically move from item to item if you have Auto Scanning enabled.

You can make use of these default gestures with the use of Auto Scanning;

- **Bring up the action menu**: Pinch
- **Reverse direction**: Double pinch
- A clench or double clench while making use of Auto Scanning will perform the action that you have given to those gestures.

Use the Confirm with AssistiveTouch feature

You can make use of AssistiveTouch to complete a double click on your Apple Watch side button, like when you confirm payment with the use of Apple Pay or unlock your Mac.

- Launch the **Settings application on your Apple Watch**.
- Touch **Accessibility > AssistiveTouch.**
- Touch **Confirm with Assistive Touch then touch Continue.**
- Click **twice on the side button, then insert your passcode**.
- Click **twice on the side button once more to confirm.**

Navigate your Apple Watch with the motion pointer

Utilizing the motion pointer with AssistiveTouch is an additional method. You may change the motion pointer by tilting your Apple Watch, which displays as a circle icon on the watch's display. Shaking your wrist or selecting an option from the action menu will start the motion pointer.

To activate the motion pointer by shaking your wrist, follow the steps below;

- Touch **Settings > Accessibility > Assistive Touch > Motion Pointer > Dwell Control.**
- Choose **Shake to start to switch on the feature.**
- Lift your Apple Watch, then shake your Wrist to ensure that the motion pointer is displayed.

To activate the motion pointer with the use of the action menu, follow the steps below;

- Raise the action menu with the use of a hand gesture. The default gesture is a double clench.
- Go forward in the action menu with the use of the default pinch gesture until Interaction is chosen, then touch it **by clenching your fist.**
- Touch **Motion Pointer.**

You can tap an object with a hand gesture when the motion cursor is moved over it and hovers over it. Alternatively, you can set a timer for the motion cursor to automatically select the object. The action menu can be configured to appear when the motion pointer selects an item on your screen. You can swipe on your Apple Watch's screen with hot edges with the motion pointer. Swipes are made in that direction when you move the motion pointer close to the edge of your screen. Under **Accessibility > AssistiveTouch > Motion Pointer, you can modify these hot edges.**

Use the AssistiveTouch action menu

You can execute actions in all regions of your Apple Watch by tapping one of the options in the action menu. The context-aware action menu adapts to the way you're using your Apple Watch by displaying the appropriate actions. Use the hand gesture that corresponds to the action menu to access it (a double clench is the default). Following that, utilize motions to tap an item and forward or rewind the list of items.

Select **Settings > Accessibility > AssistiveTouch > Customize Menu** to change the **AssistiveTouch action menu's appearance**. If so, you can:

- Touch **Add Action beneath Favorites**, then touch an action that you would like to show in the action menu along with the default items.
- Make a choice of where you would like to have the action menu displayed.
- Switch **on a larger-sized menu**.

Use Autoscroll in the action menu

With auto-scroll, you may swipe up or down on your watch's display or turn the Digital Crown with hand movements.

- Show the action menu with the use of your hand gesture. The default gesture is a double clench.
- Go forward in the action menu with the use of the default pinch gesture until Autoscroll is chosen, then touch **it by clenching your fist.**
- Make **use of the pinch gesture** to go through the Autoscroll options, then **clench your fist to choose one.**

Context-sensitive auto scroll actions will adjust to what is displayed on your screen. For instance, choosing Digital Crown in an audio app increases the volume. Instructions for using the Auto Scroll feature appear on the screen as you use it.

The Art of Force Touch and Haptic Feedback

The Apple Watch has the ability to tap out the time on your wrist with some distinct touches when it is in silent mode.

Get the following done;

- Launch the **Settings application on your Apple Watch**.
- Choose **Clock, navigate down, and then choose Taptic Time.**

- Switch On **Haptic Time**, then select **your preferred settings- Digit**s, **Terse, or Morse code. Hours and minutes are shown in the following ways;**
  - o **Digits**: Apple Watch long touches for every 10 hours, short taps for every following hour, long taps for every 10 minutes, and then short taps for every following minute.
  - o **Terse**: Apple Watch long taps for every five hours, short taps for the rest hours, and then long taps for every quarter hour.
  - o **Morse code**: Apple Watch touches each digit of the time in Morse code.
- To have a feel of a haptic version of the time, touch and hold two fingers on the watch face.

Taptic Time also works well when the Always on Display is dimmed. If the VoiceOver is turned on, switch on Taptic Time by tapping the watch face twice while the display is inactive. You can also set Taptic Time on the iPhone. Launch the Apple Watch application on your iPhone, touch **My Watch, navigate to Clock > Taptic Time, and then switch it on.** It is worth noting that Taptic Time is disabled if the Apple Watch is configured to always speak the time. To be able to make use of Taptic Time, navigate to **Settings > Clock, and then switch on Control with Silent Mode beneath Speak Time.**

Activity

1. Experiment with the use of both the digital crown and the side button.
2. Make use of the various screen gestures.
3. Configure Haptic Feedback on your watch.

CHAPTER 3
PERSONALIZING YOUR WATCH FACE

The Apple Watch comes with diverse watch faces most of which can be customized by the user of the watch in line with their preference. **Below are some of the various watch faces you can choose to set as default;**

- **Activity Analog**: this watch face displays your activity progress, superimposed over a traditional analog clock. You are at liberty to make a choice of seeing your Activity rings in the familiar stacked design or even as subdials. In this face, the customizable features include; color, and style (rings, subdials). Some of the available complications include; activity, alarms, astronomy, audiobooks, battery, blood oxygen, calculator, calendar, ECG, contacts, mail, maps, sleep, stocks, stopwatch, tips, voice memos, walkie-talkie, weather, workout, and lots more.

- **Activity Digital**: this watch face helps to display the time in a digital format alongside your various activity progress. The customizable features here include color and seconds of time. Some of the available complications are activity, alarms, astronomy, camera remote, cellular, compass, compass waypoints, heart rate, medications, messages, timer, tips, walkie-talkie, workout, world clock, and lots more.

- **Artist:** This face is quite visually engaging. It algorithmically alters every time you touch the display, and there are various combinations.

- **Astronomy**: This watch face displays a continuously updating 3D model of the Earth, moon, or the solar system. Touch the watch face, then navigate the Digital Crown to move either forward or backward in time on Earth, display the phases of the moon, or see the placement of the planet of the solar system.

The next moonrise or moonset time can be seen by adding the Moon complication to a watch face corner that already has it. For instance, 11:44 PM, 12H 4M says that the moon **will set below the horizon at your location at 11:44 in the evening, or 12 hours and 4 minutes from now.**

- **Breathe**: this watch face helps encourage you to relax and breathe mindfully. All you have to do is touch the display to commence.

- **California**: This watch comprises a mix of Roman and Arabic numerals.
- **Chronograph**: this watch face helps with the measurement of time in precise increments, such as a classic analog stopwatch. It has a stopwatch that can be activated straight from the face.
- **Chronograph Pro**: touch the outer edge that surrounds the main 12-hour dial on this watch face, and it changes into a chronograph. Document time on scales of 60, 30, 6, or 3 seconds. Or you can choose the tachymeter timescale to effectively measure speed based on time travel over a fixed distance.
- **Color**: this watch face shows the time and any other feature you choose to include in your choice of bright colors.
- **Contour**: this watch face slowly modifies to display the current hour. The numerals are a custom font designed to fit into the edge of the display and follow seamlessly from one hour to the next. Tap the watch face, then twist the Digital Crown in order to make the numbers bigger than the current hour.
- **Count Up**: the watch face can be used in the tracking of elapsed time.
- **Explorer:** this watch face prominently features green dots, which show cellular signal strength.
- **Fire and Water:** this watch face animates anytime you lift your wrist or touch the display.
- **GMT**: this watch face has two different dials; a 12-hour inner display that shows local time, and a 24-hour outer dial that enables you to track a second time zone. If you would like to configure another time zone, touch the watch face, then switch the Digital Crown to select a time zone. Touch the clock icon in order to confirm your choice and go back to the watch face. The red hand displays the hour in the second time zone.
- **Gradient**: this watch face has gradients that move with time.
- **Infograph**: this watch face has about eight rich, full-color complications and subdials.
- **Kaleidoscope**: choose a picture to design a watch face with an evolving pattern of shapes and colors. Touch the watch face then twist the Digital Crown to alter the pattern.
- **Lunar**: this watch face shows the exact relationship of the date and time to the phases of the moon. Touch the watch face, then twist the Digital Crown to go ahead or back in time.

- **Memoji**: this watch face has the Memoji you have designed and all the Memoji characters.
- **Metropolitan**: this classic, type-driven watch face features custom-designed numbers that dynamically alter in style and weight when you touch the watch face, and then twist the Digital Crown. The numerals will then rotate to pills when your wrist is down.
- **Mickey Mouse and Minnie Mouse**: allow Mickey Mouse or Minnie Mouse to offer you a whimsical view of the time- their arms rotate to show the hours and minutes, while their feet tap out every second. If you would like to hear Mickey Mouse or Minnie Mouse tell you the time, launch the Settings application on your Apple Watch, touch Clock, and then switch on Speak Time. Lift your wrist then position two fingers on the watch face to hear the time.
- **Modular**: this watch face comprises six complication slots in an easy-to-read typographic interface.
- **Modular Compact**: with the use of this watch face, you can pick about three complications as well as a digital or analog dial.
- **Modular Duo**: This watch face includes up to three complications in addition to digital time. Two of them are sizable, rectangular choices that enable you to see more specifics regarding the issues that matter to you the most.
- **Motion**: this watch face shows a very beautiful animated theme.
- **Nike Analog**: this face is designed in sync with Nike, this analog-style watch face prominently shows the time in large numerals.
- **Nike Bounce**: You can move with this watch face. Every movement you make with your wrist causes the digital numbers to move in response. To start things moving, you simply tap the screen or turn the Digital Crown.
- **Nike Digital**: This digital-style face, created in collaboration with Nike, prominently displays the clock and has a built-in complication for opening the Nike Run Club app.
- **Nike Hybrid:** The designs on this watch face are analog, digital, and Windrunner-inspired. It has up to five complexities and is highly customizable.
- **Numerals**: The designs on this watch face are analog, digital, and Windrunner-inspired. It has up to five complexities and is highly customizable.

- **Palette**: This uses dynamic color to show diverse elements of the watch face. Gradients go after the hands and alter as the second hand sweeps around the face.
- **Photos:** this watch face shows a new photo each time you lift your wrist or touch the display. Make a choice of an album, memory, or up to 24 custom pictures.
- **Playtime:** this watch face is a dynamic piece of art that is quite unique to the Apple Watch. Rotating the Digital Crown alters the background, and the characters give a reaction when you touch the face.
- **Portraits**: Your iPhone's photo collection is used for the Portraits watch face. Photos of people, dogs, cats, and landscapes all use layer effects. You can select up to 24 pictures and one of three different typefaces. Every time you lift your wrist or tap the display, a fresh image shows.
- **Siri**: this face shows information that is quite helpful and timely. It might be your next appointment, the traffic on the way to your house, or the time the sun sets, and you can also touch it to get more information. Twist the Digital Crown to navigate through your day. Tap the Digital Crown to go back to the watch face.
- **Snoopy**: This watch face, which features the well-known beagle Snoopy, exemplifies the playful nature of the Peanuts dog. Snoopy engages in conversation with Woodstock and the watch hands. By selecting the Sunday Surprise color setting, the background changes colors every Sunday in a nod to Sunday comic strips.
- **Solar Dial**: this watch face has a 24-hour, circular dial that checks the sun as well as an analog or digital one that goes opposite the path of the sun.

Watch Face Selection and Customization

The face gallery in the Apple Watch application is the easiest way to have a view of all of the available watch faces. When you locate one that seems enticing to you, you can customize it, choose complications, and then include the face in your collection all from the gallery.

Open the Face Gallery

Open the Apple Watch application on your iPhone, and touch the Face Gallery at the lower part of the screen.

Choose features for a face

In the Face Gallery, touch a face, then touch a feature like color or style. As you use various options, the face at the upper part will change so you will be sure that the design is just the perfect one for you.

Add complications in the Face Gallery

- In the Face Gallery, touch **a face**, then touch a **complication position, like Top Left, Top Right, or Bottom.**
- Swipe to view the exact complications that are available in that particular place, then choose the one you prefer.
- If you make a decision that you do not want a complication in that position, navigate **to the top of the list and touch Off**.

Add a face

- In the Face Gallery, touch **a face,** and then make **a choice of the features and the very complications you wish for.**
- Touch **Add**. The face will then be included in your collection and it will then become the current face on your Apple Watch.

Customize the watch face

Create a customized Apple Watch face with the features you require and the appearance you choose. Select a design, alter the color and other details, and then include it in your collection. Change faces whenever necessary to view the proper timekeeping equipment or to stir things up. The simplest way to view all of the watch faces that are offered, customize one, and add it to your collection is through the Face Gallery in the Apple Watch app. However, you can change the watch face directly on your watch if your iPhone is not nearby.

Choose another watch face

Touch and hold the watch face, swipe to the one you would like to make use of, and then touch it. You can also choose to add some special features known as complications to some watch faces. With this, you will be able to check things immediately like stock prices, the weather report, or information from other applications that you have installed.

- With the watch face displaying, touch the **hold the display, and then choose Edit.**

- Move to the left all the way to the end. If for any reason a face gives complications, they will be displayed on the last screen.
- Touch a complication to choose it, then switch **the Digital Crown** to choose another one like activity or heart rate.
- Once you are done, tap **the Digital Crown to keep your changes**, then **touch the face to turn to it.**

Complication options on Apple Watch

You can launch most applications by touching a complication on the watch face. Certain complications display certain information from a specific application so you are able to view just the things you need at just a glance. Weather, for instance, has complications for air quality, conditions, temperature, and lots more. Applications that provide various complications include; activity, time, stocks, sleep, maps, home, compass waypoints, timer, world clock, calendar, compass, etc.

Add a watch face to your collection

Design your collection of custom faces as well as variations of the same design.

- With the current watch face being displayed, touch and hold **the display**.
- Move left all the way to the end, and then touch the **New button (+).**

- Turn **the Digital Crown to check watch faces**, and then touch **Add.**

You can choose to touch a collection like New Watch Faces or Artists if you would like to browse a certain category of watch faces. Once you have added it you can then proceed to personalizing it to suit your preference.

Viewing your collection

You can view all of your watch faces at the slightest glance. Follow the steps below to get this done;

- Open the **Apple Watch app on your phone.**
- Touch **My Watch** then proceed to swiping through all of your collection beneath **My Faces.**

If you would like to rearrange the order of your collection, touch **Edit in My Faces**, then move close to either a watch face up or down. The arrangement of your collection can also be changed on Apple Watch. Drag the selected watch face left or right while the current watch face is visible by touching and holding the display twice.

Deleting a face from your collection

- With the current face being displayed, touch and h**old the display.**
- Swipe to the face you would like to delete, swipe it up, then touch **Remove.**

As against the above, you can choose to make use of your iPhone, open the Apple Watch app, touch **My Watch, and then touch Edit in the My Faces area**. Touch the red circle close to the watch faces you would like to delete, then touch **Remove**. Though deleted, you can always choose to add the watch face again much later if need be.

Share Apple Watch Faces

With pals, you can exchange watch faces. The complications built within watchOS as well as those made by outside developers can be integrated into shared faces.

Note: The watch face's recipient must likewise own an Apple Watch running watchOS 7 or above.

The set of instructions below will help you with sharing a watch face;

- On the Apple Watch, display **the watch face you would like to share.**
- Touch and hold **the display, and then touch the share icon.**
- Touch the name of the watch face, then touch **"Don't include" for any complications that you would not like to share.**
- Touch **a recipient, or touch Messages or Mail. If you touch Messages or Mail, add a contact, subject (Mail), and message.**
- Touch **Send.**

You can also launch the Apple Watch app, touch a watch face from your collection or Face Gallery, touch the share icon then pick a sharing option.

Receiving a watch face

Sharing and receiving are of course the opposite of one another. When you share you need to also learn how to receive and this is what this section is about. Shared watches can be received by messages by mail, or by selecting a link online.

- Open **a text, email, or link that has a shared watch face.**
- Touch the shared watch face, then touch **Add.**

If a third-party app sends you a watch face with a complication, press the price of the app or download the app from the App Store. To get the watch face without the third-party complication, press Continue without This App as well.

Time Travel, and Timekeeping Enhancements

You can use the time travel option to see what is in store for your day. Compatible complications will indicate their status at the moment you choose when you move the Digital Crown while your watch face is on display. Use the Weather complication as an illustration, and it will display the current temperature. The complication will display the weather at that moment if you use time travel to scroll one hour in the future. Keep in mind that not all difficulties work with time travel. If it doesn't support time travel, the complications icon will fade. In the Activity complication, for instance, you may scroll backward to see how much progress you made earlier in the day, but if you go forward, the symbol will darken because it is unable to estimate your progress later in the day. You can travel through time by going backward up to the start of the day before or ahead; up to the end of the day after. Grab your iPhone and head to **Watch > Notifications > Clock > Time Travel to activate it.**

Alarms, Timers, and World Clocks

Almost everyone around the world makes use of the alarm. It is very useful and helps to ensure that one is always in check as regards whatever one wants to do. Alarms oftentimes are configured on the phone but with the use of your Apple Watch, you can also set an alarm. With the Apple Watch, you can use the Alarm application to play a sound or vibrate your Apple Watch at a certain period of time.

Alarm

Set an alarm on your Apple Watch

- Open the **Alarms application on your Apple Watch.**

- Touch **the add icon.**

- Choose **between AM and PM, then configure the hours and minutes. This step is quite necessary when you are making use of the 24-hour time.**
- Switch **the Digital Crown to modify, then proceed.**
- If you would like to either switch on or off the alarm, touch **its switch.** You can also choose to touch the alarm to configure repeat, label, and the various snooze options.

When an alarm sounds, you can choose to touch snooze so that the alarm pauses for some minutes before it eventually comes on once more.

If you do not have a need to snooze, follow the steps below;

- Launch **the Alarms application on your Apple Watch.**
- Touch **the alarm in the list of alarms, then switch off Snooze.**

Deleting an Alarm

- Launch **the Alarms application on your Apple Watch.**
- Touch **the specific alarm you would like to delete from the list.**
- Navigate **to the bottom, then touch Delete.**

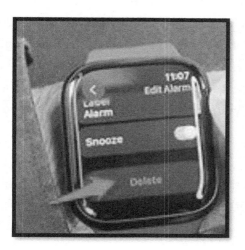

Skip a wake-up alarm

If you have an alarm that helps you get out of bed as a part of your sleep schedule, you can choose to skip it for an evening. To get this done simply;

- Open **the Alarms application on your Apple Watch.**
- Touch **the alarm that is displayed beneath Alarms**, then touch **Skip for Tonight.** Once done you can get to enjoy your sleep for much longer hours.

See the same alarms on both iPhone and Apple Watch

- Configure **the alarm on your iPhone.**
- Launch **the Apple Watch application on your iPhone.**
- Touch **My Watch, touch the clock, and then switch on Push Alerts from the iPhone.**

Your Apple Watch will then alert you whenever an alarm goes off so you will be able to snooze or dismiss the alarm. Note that you will not be alerted on your phone when your Apple Watch alarm goes off.

Set up the Apple Watch as a nightstand clock with an alarm

- Open the **Settings application on your Apple Watch.**
- Locate **General > Nightstand Mode, then switch on Nightstand Mode.**

The time of any alarms you've set, the date, and the current time are all displayed when you plug your Apple Watch into its charger and activate bedside mode. Tap the screen or give your Apple Watch a gentle push to view the time. Even tapping or bumping the table might be effective. You can use the side button to silence the alarm when it goes off or the Digital Crown to snooze it for an additional nine minutes if you set an alarm using the Alarms app while wearing your Apple Watch in nightstand mode.

Timers

The Timers application on the Apple Watch can be of immense help in tracking time. You can configure various timers that can help with tracking time for about 24 hours.

Setting a timer

- Open the **Timers application on your Apple Watch.**

- If you would like to swiftly commence a timer, touch your preferred duration like 1,3, or even 5 minutes or you can choose to touch a timer you have used recently under Recents. If you would like to design a custom timer, touch **its icon.**

Whenever a timer goes off, you can touch the restart icon for the timer of the same duration to commence again.

Pause or end a timer

You can always pause or completely end a timer if you do not have a need for it anymore. To get this done, follow the steps below;

- With a timer being used currently, open the **Timers application on your Apple Watch.**
- Tap **the pause icon to pause the timer, touch the play icon to resume, or touch the X icon to completely end the timer.**

Create a personalized custom timer

- Open **the Timers application on your Apple Watch.**
- Touch **the add icon.**

- Choose **your preferred number of hours, minutes, or seconds; switch the Digital Crown to adjust.**
- Finally, touch **Start.**

Creating multiple timers

- Open **the Timers application on your Apple Watch.**
- Design and start a timer. If you would like to assign a label like "Football" to a timer, make use of Siri to create the timer. Simply lift your Apple Watch, then say something like "Set a 30-minute Football timer".
- Touch **the add icon** to go back to the **Timers screen**, then create and commence **another timer.** Touch the backward arrow to show your running timers on the Timers screen. Touch the pause icon if you would like to pause a timer, and then touch the play icon to resume the timer. If you would like to delete a running or paused timer that shows on the Timers screen, swipe left and then touch the **X icon.**

World Clock

In a world where people love to travel and migrate from one country to another, having a world clock at one's disposal is something everyone would love to jump at. In this section, you will learn how to operate the world clock.

Add and remove cities in World Clock

- Launch the **World Clock application on your Apple Watch.**
- Tap **the add city icon.**

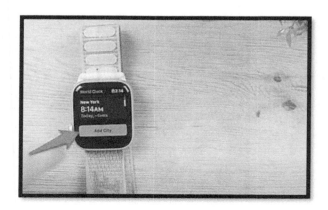

- Insert **the name of the city**, or make use of Scribble or dictation to insert the city name. To make use of Scribble, swipe up from the lower part of the screen, then touch Scribble. It is worth noting that Scribble is not available in every language.
- Touch **the name of the city to include it in the World Clock.**

If you would like to remove a city, swipe to its left on its name in the list of the cities, then touch **X.** The cities you include on your iPhone will also be displayed in World Clock on your Apple Watch.

Check the time in another city

- Open the **World Clock** application on your Apple Watch.
- Turn the **Digital Crown** or you can also choose to swipe to **navigate through the list.**
- To have more information about a particular city which includes the time of sunrise and sunset, touch the city in the list.
- When you are done, touch the backward arrow in the top-left corner, or you can also make a choice of swiping right to go back to the list of cities.

Change city abbreviations

If you would like to alter a city abbreviation used on your Apple Watch, follow the following steps below;

- Open the **Apple Watch application on your phone.**
- Touch **My Watch, then go to Clock > City Abbreviations.**
- Touch **any city to alter its abbreviation.**

Activity

1. What are Complications? Mention 3 of the complications highlighted in this book and state their uses.
2. Activate Time travel on your watch.
3. Check out world clocks and also configure Alarms on your watch.

CHAPTER 4
STAYING CONNECTED

Staying connected when making use of the Apple Watch Series 9 provides various benefits and advantages that help with the enhancement of an overall experience with the device and one's daily life. When you remain connected, you get real-time notifications coming directly from your wrist for messages, calls, emails, calendar events, and application updates. With this, you remain informed without having to keep checking your phone, ensuring it becomes more convenient and efficient. For the sake of communication (if that alone), it is of extreme importance that you remain connected as this allows you to make calls and send messages in case of an emergency and also when you are at a place where you are unable to reach your phone. In this chapter, you will learn more about remaining connected with the use of a notification center, dealing with calls, emailing, and sending text messages all from your Apple Watch!

The Notification Center Demystified

Applications have the ability to deliver notifications to keep you updated; meeting invitations, messages, noise alerts, and activity reminders are just a few examples. If you don't read a notice right away, it's saved so you can check it later on your Apple Watch, which can show notifications as they come in.

Respond to a notification when it arrives

- If you are able to hear or feel a notification, lift your wrist to see it. The look of the notification is based on whether the display is active or idle.
  - **Active display**: a little banner showing at the upper part of the display.
  - **Idle display**: a full-screen notification will be displayed.
- Touch the notification so you are able to read it.
- If you have a need to clear a notification, navigate downwards on it. Or move to the lower part of the notification, then touch **Dismiss.**

See notifications you have not responded to

If you do not reply to a notification when you get it, it will be saved in the Notification Center. A red dot at the upper part of the face of your watch will show when you have an unread notification.

To see this, follow the steps below;

- Directly from the face of the watch, move down to the **Notification Center**. From other screens, touch and hold th**e upper part of the screen, then move downwards.**
  It is worth noting however that you cannot open the Notification Center when you are seeing the Home Screen on your Apple Watch. Rather, touch the **Digital Crown to locate the watch face or you can also choose to open an application and then open the Notification Center.**
- Move upwards or downwards or you can also choose to switch the **Digital Crown to move through the list of notifications.**
- Touch **the notification to read or to provide a response to it.**

Note that Siri has the capacity to read the notifications in the Notification Center to your hearing; either through the Apple Watch speaker or through headphones that have been connected to Bluetooth. All you have to do is say "Read my notifications". If you would like to clear a certain notification from the Notification Center without you getting to read it, swipe the notification to the left, then **touch X**. If you would like to clear all notifications. Move to the upper part of the screen and choose **Clear All.** If you do not like the red dot being displayed on the watch face, launch the **Settings application on your Apple Watch, touch Notifications, and then turn off the Notification indicator.**

Silence all notifications on the Apple Watch

Tap the side button to launch the Control Center, then touch the bell icon. You will still feel a tap when you get a notification. If you would like to keep the sound and taps silent, follow the steps below;

- Tap **the side button to launch Control Center**, then touch the **crescent icon or the active Focus.**

- Touch **Do Not Disturb,** then make a choice of an option; On, On for 1 hour, or On until this evening/On until tomorrow morning.

It is worth noting that whenever you receive a notification, you can swiftly mute your Apple Watch by simply resting the palm of your hand on the watch display for a minimum of three seconds. You will then feel a tap that helps you to confirm that mute is already on. Ensure Cover to mute is switched on; launch the Settings application on your Apple Watch, touch Sounds & Haptics then switch on Cover to Mute.

Change notification settings on the Apple Watch

By default, the settings for notification for the various applications on an Apple Watch that you configure for yourself show the configurations on your iPhone. Nevertheless, you can also choose to customize how certain applications show notifications. It is worth noting that settings that are mirrored do not in any way apply to an Apple Watch you manage for a family member.

Choose how applications send notifications

- Open the **Apple Watch on your iPhone**.
- Touch **My Watch, then choose Notifications.**
- Touch the application, for instance, messages, then touch Custom, then choose your preferred option. The options available may include;
  - **Allow Notifications**: The application shows notifications in the Notification Center.
  - **Send to Notification Center**: Notifications are usually sent directly to the Notification Center without your Apple Watch making any kind of sound or showing the notification.
  - **Notifications Off**: the application transfers no notifications.
- **Notification grouping: Make a choice of just how notifications for the applications are being grouped. The various options include;**
  - **Off**: Notifications are not grouped.
  - **Automatically**: Your Apple Watch makes use of diverse information from the application for the creation of different groups. For instance, News

notifications are grouped by the channels you follow like CNN, Washington Post, etc.

- ○ **By App**: All of the notifications of the applications are grouped.

Some apps allow you to customize the type of notifications you receive. For example, in Calendar, you can restrict notifications to specific calendars or actions, such as when you receive an invitation or someone modifies a shared calendar. You may specify which email accounts are allowed to deliver notifications in the Mail.

Change notifications settings directly on your Apple Watch

You can choose to manage other notification preferences directly on your Apple Watch by moving to the left on a notification and touching the more options.

Below are the various options available;

- **Mute 1 hour or Mute for Today**: For the next hour or probably for the rest of the day, notifications will be sent directly to the Notification Center without any sound coming from your Apple Watch not showing the notification. If you would like to have a view and also hear these notification alerts once more, move to the left on a notification, touch ***, then touch **Unmute.**

- **Add to summary**: Future notifications from the application display in the Notification Summary on your iPhone.
If you would like to have the application notify you instantly, launch the Settings application on your iPhone, touch **Notifications, touch the application, and then choose Immediate Delivery.**

- **Turn off Time Settings**: Time-sensitive notifications are usually sent instantly, even if you are making use of a Focus that delays most notifications. Nevertheless, if you would like to prevent this app from being able to deliver even notifications that are time-sensitive instantly, touch **this option**.

- **Turn off:** The application sends no notifications. To get notifications reenabled from the application, launch the Apple Watch app on your iPhone, **touch My Watch, touch Notifications, touch the specific app you would like to adjust, and then touch Allow Notifications.**

Show notifications on the lock screen

You can make a choice of how notifications should be displayed on the lock screen of your Apple Watch.

- Launch the S**ettings application on your Apple Watch.**
- Touch **Notifications.**
- **Make a choice of any of the following options;**
    - **Show Summary When Locked**: When you enable this option, your Apple Watch displays a notification summary—or brief look—when it is locked. The summary comprises the name and emblem of the alerting app, as well as a brief headline.
    - **Tap to Show Full Notification**: When you lift your wrist to view a notice, you will first see a brief summary, followed by full details a few seconds later. For instance, when a message arrives, you first see who sent it, and then the message shows. Turn this option on to prevent the whole notification from displaying unless you tap it.
    - **Show Notifications on Wrist Down**: When your wrist is down, notifications on your Apple Watch do not appear by default. Turn on this option to get notifications even when your Apple Watch is turned away from you.

Handling Calls on Your Apple Watch

Make a Call

- Launch **the Phone application on your Apple Watch.**
- Touch **Contacts**, then switch **the Digital Crown to scroll.**
- Touch **the contact you would like to call**, then touch **the phone button.**
- Touch **FaceTime Audio to commence a FaceTime audio call, and touch a phone number.**
- Turn **the Digital Crown to modify the volume while a call is ongoing.**

If you would like to put a call through to someone you have just spoken to, touch Recents, and then touch **Contact**. If you would like to call a person you have designated as a favorite in the Phone app on your iPhone, touch Favorites, and then touch a contact.

Make a Group FaceTime call

With the use of the Apple Watch Series 9, you can make Group FaceTime audio calls on your watch...amazing right! Follow the steps below to learn how to do this;

- Launch **the Phone app on your Apple Watch**.
- Commence **a FaceTime audio call.**
- If you would like to bring more people on the call, get one of the following done;
    - Touch the **More option,** touch **Add People**, and then **make a choice of contact.**
    - If a person has joined the call, touch **2 People Active**, touch **the add icon at the lower part of the screen, and then make a choice of a contact.**

If you happen to be on the call but did not start it, you can also include another person. Touch **2 People Active**, touch **the add icon,** then **make a choice of a contact, or touch Add People, then choose your preferred contact.**

Insert a phone number on your Apple Watch

- Open **the Phone application on your Apple Watch**.
- Commence **a FaceTime audio call.**
- Touch **the more options,** then touch **Add People.**

You can also choose to make use of the keypad to insert more digits while a call is ongoing. All you have to do is touch **the more option,** then touch the **Keypad button.**

Make calls over Wi-Fi

If your cellular provider supports Wi-Fi calling, you can use your Apple Watch to make and receive calls via Wi-Fi rather than the cellular network—even if your associated iPhone isn't nearby or is turned off. Your Apple Watch only needs to be within range of a Wi-Fi network that your iPhone has previously connected to.

- On your iPhone, locate **Settings > Phone, touch Wi-Fi Calling, then switch on both Wi-Fi Calling on This iPhone and Add Wi-Fi Calling for Other Devices.**
- Launch **the Phone application on your Apple Watch.**

- Make **a choice of a contact, then touch the call icon**.
- Choose **the phone number or FaceTime address you would like to call.**

You can make emergency calls over Wi-Fi, but if at all possible, use your iPhone over a cellular connection—your location information will be more accurate.

See call info on Apple Watch

While you are speaking on your iPhone, you are able to see call information on your Apple Watch in the Phone application. You can also make a choice of ending the call from your Apple Watch (for instance, if you are making use of an earphone or a headset).

Answer a call

When you hear or have a feeling of the call notification, lift your wrist to view who is calling you.

- **Send a call to voicemail**: Touch **the end button in the incoming call notification.**
- **Answer on your Apple Watch**: Touch **the receive butto**n to talk with the built-in microphone and speaker or a Bluetooth device paired with your Apple Watch.
- **Answer using your iPhone or send a text message instead**: Touch **the more option,** then touch **your preferred option**. If you touch Answer on your iPhone, the call will be placed on hold and the caller will hear a repeated sound until you answer on your paired iPhone.

While you are on a call

If you're on a call that doesn't use FaceTime audio, you can switch to your iPhone, change the call volume, enter digits using the keypad, and switch the conversation to another audio source.

- **Switch a call from your Apple Watch to your iPhone**: While speaking on your Apple Watch, unlock **your iPhone**, then touch t**he green button or the bar at the upper part of the screen.**

You can quickly silence an incoming call by tapping the palm of your hand on the watch display for about three seconds. All you have to do is ensure you have Cover to Mute switched on; open the **Settings application** on your Apple Watch, touch **Sounds & Haptics, and then switch on Cover to Mute.**

- **Adjust call volume**: Switch **the Digital Crown.** Touch **the mute icon** to mute your aspect of the call. This works well if you are on a conference call for instance.
- **Insert more digits during a call:** Touch **the more options**, touch the **Keypad**, and then touch **the various digits you would like to add.**
- **Switch the call to an audio device**: Touch **the more option**, then **make a choice of your preferred device.**

While a FaceTime audio call is ongoing, you can choose to modify the volume, mute the call by touching the mute icon, or touch the more option, and make a choice of an audio destination.

Listen to voicemail

You'll receive a notification if a caller leaves a voicemail; hit the Play button in the notification to listen. Open the Phone app on your Apple Watch and hit Voicemail to listen to voicemail later.

On the voicemail screen, you have these options;

- Adjust volume with the Digital Crown.
- Start and stop playback.
- Skip ahead or back five seconds.
- Call back.
- Delete the voicemail
- Read a transcription of the voicemail.

Texting and iMessage Tricks

Read incoming text messages in the Messages app on Apple Watch, then respond with dictation, Scribble, emoji, or a preset response; type a reply using the QWERTY and QuickPath keyboard (on compatible models only, not accessible in all languages); or go to your iPhone to make a response.

Read a message on the Apple Watch

- Whenever you feel a tap or you hear an alert sound informing you that a message has arrived, lift your **Apple Watch to read the message**.
- Switch the **Digital Crown** to move to the lower part of the message.
- If you would like to get to the upper part of the message, touch **the upper part of the screen.**

You can touch the link of a website within a message to see web-formatted content being optimized for Apple Watch. Click **twice to zoom in on the content.** If the message came in moments ago, tap and hold **the upper part of the screen**, move **down on the display to view the message notification**, and then **touch it**. If you would like to have the message marked as being read, move down, then touch **Dismiss.** To dismiss the notification without having to mark the message as read, touch **the Digital Crown**. If you would like to see when messages have been sent, touch a conversation in the Messages conversation list, then move to the left on a message in the conversation.

Mute or delete a conversation

- **Mute a conversation**: Move to the left side of the conversation in the messages conversation list then touch **the mute icon**.
- **Delete a conversation**: Move to the left of the conversation in the Messages conversation list, then touch **the delete icon (symbol of a bin).**

Access photos, audio, music, and video in a message

There are times when your messages may have pictures, audio (voice notes from a loved one), and videos. If you would like to gain access to them directly from your Apple Watch, follow the steps below;

- **Photo**: Touch the photo to see it, touch twice to get the screen filled, and then move it to the pan. When you are done, touch the backward arrow sign in the top-left corner to go back to the conversation. If there is a need for you to share the photo, touch the share icon, then touch a sharing option- make a choice of people you usually send messages to, or you can choose to touch messages or mail. If you would like to store the image in the photo applications on your iPhone, go beyond the sharing options, then touch Save Image. You can also choose to touch **Create Watch Face to design a Kaleidoscope or Photos watch face with the image.**

- **Audio clip:** Touch **the clip** to listen to send audio messages. Note that immediately after two minutes, the audio clip will be deleted instantly in order to save space; if you would like to keep them, touch **Keep** underneath the clip. The audio message will remain on your watch for up to 30 days, and you can then configure it to stay much longer on your iPhone. Navigate to **Settings > Messages, and move to Audio messages, touch Expire, then touch Never.**

- **Music**: If someone has shared music from Apple Music through messages, touch the song, album, or playlist in the message to open and also play it in the Music application on your watch. Note that there is a need for an Apple Music subscription to perform this feature.

- **Video:** Touch a video in a message to commence playing the video full-screen. Touch once to show the playback controls. Touch **the screen twice to zoom out** and then switch the **Digital Crown** to modify the volume. Move or touch **the Back button to go back to the conversation**. If you would like to save the video, open the message in the Messages application on your iPhone, and have it saved there.

Delete sensitive content

You are at liberty to detect and blur photos and videos that appear to be sensitive before you see them on your Apple Watch.

- On your iPhone, navigate **to Settings > Privacy & Security, then touch Sensitive Content Warning.**
- Switch on **Sensitive Content Warning**, then ensure **AirDrop, Messages, and Video Messages are switched on.**
- If you would like to see the content after you have been warned, touch **Show,** then touch **I am sure**. To gain some knowledge on how to deal with sensitive content, touch Ways to Get Help. When you turn on this setting, it will affect images and videos on the iPhone as well as your Apple Watch. It is worth noting that Apple doesn't have access to the photos or videos.

Choose how to be notified of new messages

- Open the **Apple Watch application on your iPhone.**

- Touch **My Watch, then touch Messages**.
- Touch **Custom** to configure options for how you would like to be notified when you get a message. You will not get a notification if you are making use of a Focus that does not enable message notifications.

Send messages from the Apple Watch

You can write and send messages that include photographs, emoji, Memoji stickers, and audio snippets using the Messages app on your Apple Watch. You can also use Apple Pay to pay money and let individuals know where you are by putting your location in a message.

Create a message on the Apple Watch

- Launch **the Messages application** on your Apple Watch.
- Touch **the upper part of the screen**.
- Touch **Add Contact**, touch **a contact in the list of recent conversations that shows, or make a choice of your preferred option;**
  - Touch the record icon to dictate a phone number or to locate someone in your contacts.
  - Touch the contact icon to make a choice from your full list of contacts.
  - Tap **the number pad to insert a phone number.**
- Touch **Create Message**.
- If you have configured your Apple Watch to make use of more than just one language, touch **Language, then make a choice of a language.**

Compose a text message

You can choose to compose a message in a variety of ways; most of them on just one screen.

Once you have created a message, touch the **Create Message field**, then do at least one of the following;

- **Use the QWERTY and QuickPath keyboard**: (Only on supported models; not accessible in all languages) Enter characters by tapping them, or utilize the QuickPath keyboard to move from one letter to the next without raising your finger. Lift your finger to end a sentence.

As you type, suggested words emerge. You can also highlight a finished or unfinished word, then flip the **Digital Crown** to display recommended words. To enter the highlighted proposal, stop **twisting the Digital Crown**. If you do not see the keyboard, move up from the button, then touch the Keyboard button.

- **Use Scribble**: Write your message with your finger. To modify your message, flip the Digital Crown to position the cursor, then make your changes. Swipe up from the bottom of the screen and press **Scribble** to use Scribble on Apple Watch models that support the QWERTY and QuickPath keyboards. To use **predictive** text, highlight a finished or unfinished word, then turn the **Digital Crown** to display recommended words. To enter the highlighted proposal, **stop twisting the Digital Crown.** If you have already configured your Apple Watch to make use of more than one language, you can decide to choose another language when making use of Scribble. All you have to do is swipe up from the lower part of the screen, then make your preferred language choice. Note however that scribble is usually not always available in all languages.
- **Dictate text:** Touch **the microphone icon** then say whatever it is you would like to say, then touch **Done**.

You can talk about the addition of punctuation like "did is arrive question mark". To go back to making use of scribble, switch t**he Digital Crown**.
- **Include emoji**: Touch **an emoji icon**, then touch an emoji you usually use frequently or you can also choose to touch and hold a category at the lower part of the screen, move to the left or right to make a choice of category, then navigate to locate emojis that are available. When you are able to locate the right symbol, touch it to include it in your message.
- **Insert text with your iPhone**: When you commence creating a message and your paired iPhone is closeby, a notification will be displayed on the iPhone, enabling

you to insert text with the use of the iOS keyboard. Touch **the notification,** then type the text with the use of the keyboard of the iPhone.

Unsend a message

You can undo a message you have just sent for about two minutes after you must have sent it.

- Open the **Message application on your Apple Watch.**
- Touch and hold **the message bubble**, then touch **Undo Send**. A note that confirms that you have unsent the message will be shown in both conversation transcripts; yours and that of your recipient's. When you unsend a message, it removes the message from the device of your recipient.

If the person you are also sending the message to is making use of a device with iOS 15.7, iPadOS 15.7, macOS 12.6, and watchOS 9 or earlier, the main message will be in the conversation. When you unsend a message, you will be notified that the recipient may still see the main message in the message transcript.

Edit a sent message

You can decide to edit a recently sent message up to five times within just 15 minutes of sending it.

- Open the **Messages application** on your Apple Watch.
- Choose a conservation with the message you would like to edit.
- Tap and hold the message bubble, then touch **Edit.**
- Make any modifications, then touch **Done** to resend with edits. It is worth noting that the message is marked as edited in the conversation transcript.

The message bubble on your recipient's smartphone is updated to reflect your changes, and both of you can hit **Edited** to see prior versions of your message. If the person you're contacting is using an iOS 15.7, iPadOS 15.7, macOS 12.6, watchOS 9, or earlier device, they will get follow-up messages with the preface "Edited to" and your updated message in quote marks. Messages delivered by SMS are not editable.

Send a smart reply, Memoji sticker, sticker, GIF, or audio clip

You can also create messages without inserting a single character. Try one of the following options after creating a message;

- **Send a smart reply**: Navigate to see a list of handy phrases that you can make use of; touch one, then touch **Send**. If you would like to add your own phrase, launch the Apple Watch app on your iPhone, touch **My Watch, move to Messages > Default Replies, and then touch Add Reply**. If you would like to personalize the default replies, touch **Edit**, then move to reorder them, or touch the red icon to get one deleted. If the smart replies are not in the language you would like to make use of, move down, touch languages, and then touch a language. The languages that are available are the ones you enable on your iPhone in **Settings > General > Keyboard > Keyboards**.

Share your location in Messages on Apple Watch

In an iMessage conversation in the Message application, you can allow others to get to know where you are just by sharing your location. It is worth noting that sharing your location in Messages is not available in all of the regions.

Turn in Share My Location

- Launch the **Settings application on your Apple Watch**.
- Touch **Privacy & Security**, then touch **Location Services.**
- Touch Share My Location, then ensure **Share My Location is switched on**.
- Move down, touch Messages, and then make sure that either Ask Next Time or When I Share, or While Using the App is switched on. You are also able to locate these settings on your paired iPhone. Navigate to **Settings > Privacy & Security > Location Services > Share My Location**. In Location Services, **touch Messages and make a choice of your setting.**

Share and update your location automatically

When you share your location in a Message conversation, it can get updated in real-time right in the conversation.

- Open the **Messages application on your Apple Watch.**
- To commence a new message or open a conversation, touch **the apple icon.**
- Choose to share your live location, which updates as you progress, or share your static location.
  - **Share your live location:** Touch **Share.**
  - **Share your static location**: Tap the **notification icon and then touch the Send pin.**

The person getting your static location can touch the message to open your location in the Maps application.

- Touch **Share**, then make a choice of how long you would like to share your location. Touch in an indefinite manner if you would like to share your location until you manually stop sharing it.
- Touch **Send** if you would like to send your message. Or touch the cancel icon if you change your mind.

For them to get their location shared, your recipient can touch the message with the location in it to launch the Find People application, then touch Share.

Replying directly to one message in a conversation

In a group conversation, you can respond to a certain message in order to help ensure that the conversation is arranged.

- In a Message conversation, touch twice on a certain message to reply to, then **touch Reply.**
- Create your response, then **touch Send**. Only the person you reply to will get to see the message.

Share a message

Friends' communications frequently feature information and thoughts that you want to share with others. Follow these steps to send a message:

- In a message conversation, touch a certain message twice, then touch **Share**.
- Pick people you often exchange messages with or touch **Messages or Mail.**
- If you have chosen Messages or Mail, include contacts and, if you are sending an email, add a subject.
- Touch **Send**.

Email Management and Third-Party Messaging Applications

Read incoming mail in the Mail app on Apple Watch, then reply using dictation, Scribble, emoji, or a preset response; enter a reply using the QWERTY and QuickPath keyboards (on supported models only, not accessible in all languages); or move to your iPhone to type a response.

Read mail in a notification

- If you would like to read a message, all you have to do is raise your wrist when the notification arrives.
- If you want to dismiss the notification, swipe down from the top or touch Dismiss at the end of the message. If for any reason you happen to miss the notification, move down on the watch face later to view unread notifications, then touch it there.

To gain control of the email notifications on your Apple Watch, launch the Apple Watch application on your iPhone, touch My Watch, and then navigate to Mail > Custom.

Read mail in the Mail app

- Open the **Mail application on your Apple Watch**.
- Touch a mailbox, then switch **the Digital Crown** to move through the list of messages.
- Touch **a message to read it.**

- If you would like to jump to the top of a long message, touch t**he top of the screen**.

Messages are formatted to be seen on your Apple Watch. Most text styles are preserved, and you can touch website links in Mail and see web-formatted content optimized for Apple Watch. Click **twice to zoom in on the content.** Note also that website links may not be available in all regions. You can make a call, open a map, or see web-formatted content from a mail message by touching a phone number, address, or link.

Switch to iPhone

When you get a message you would like to read on your iPhone, go through the steps below;

- Wake your **iPhone.**
- On an **iPhone with Face ID,** move up from the lower edge and pause to display the App Switcher. On an iPhone with a Home button, tap twice on the Home button to display the App Switcher.
- Touch **the button** at the lower part of the screen to **launch Mail.**

Write and reply to mail on your Apple Watch

Create a message

- Launch the **Mail app on your Apple Watch.**
- Touch the **top left of the Mailboxes screen** and at the lower right of other screens.
- Touch **Add Contact to include a recipient,** tap **From** to make a choice of an account to send from, touch **Add Subject** to design a subject line, and then touch **Create Message.**

Reply to message on Apple Watch

Navigate to the lower part of a message you received in the Mail application then touch the reply icon. If there is more than one recipient, touch Reply All. **Once done, do any of the following;**

- **Send a smart reply**: Navigate to have a view of suggested phrases that you can make use of; just touch one to send it. To include a phrase of your own, open the **Apple Watch application on your iPhone, touch My Watch, navigate to Mail > Default Replies, and then touch Reply**. If you would like to customize the default replies, touch **Edit**, then move to have them rearranged or touch the delete icon to have one of them deleted. If the suggested replies are not in the language you would like to make use of, navigate down, touch Languages, and then touch your preferred language. The languages that are available are those that are allowed on your **iPhone in Settings > General > Keyboard > Keyboards.**
- **Compose a reply**: Touch the **Add Message field,** then create a reply.

Open the email on the iPhone

- If you would like to send the reply on your iPhone, wake your iPhone, then launch the App Switcher. (On an iPhone with Face ID, move up from the lower edge and pause a little; on an iPhone with the use of a Home button, tap twice on the Home button.
- Touch the button that displays at the lower part of the screen to have the email in Mail opened.

Manage mail on Apple Watch

Choose which mailboxes appear on the Apple Watch

- Launch the **Apple Watch app** on your iPhone.
- Touch **My Watch, then navigate to Mail > Include Mail.**
- Touch the accounts you would like to have on your Apple Watch beneath Accounts. You can choose to indicate more than one account; for instance, iCloud, and the account you use at work (Gmail for example).
- If need be, touch an account, then indicate mailboxes to have a view of their contents on your Apple Watch.

By default, you will be able to view messages from all inboxes. You can also make a choice to see messages from VIPs, flagged messages, unread messages, and lots more. You can also make a choice of the accounts and mailboxes you would like to see on your Apple Watch. Launch the Mail app, move down, touch Edit, then touch an account or mailbox.

View specific accounts on the Apple Watch

- Open the **Mail app on your Apple Watch.**
- Touch **the left arrow icon** in the top-left corner to have a view of the list of accounts and special mailboxes, like **Flagged and Unread.**
- Touch **an account or mailbox to see the contents in it.**

If you would like to see your email from all accounts, touch **All inboxes.**

Delete, mark as unread or read, or flag a message

Launch the Mail application on your Apple Watch, open a mail message, and then navigate to the lower part;

- **Mark a message unread or read**: Touch **"Mark as Unread"** or **"Mark as Read"**. If you have a view of the message list, move to the right on the message, then touch the **Read or Unread button.**
- **Delete a message**: Touch **Trash Message**. If you happen to be looking at the list of messages, move to the left on the message then touch the delete icon.
- **Flag a message:** Touch **Flag (Note that you can also choose to unflag an already flagged message)**. If you are having a view of the message list, move to the left of the message and then touch the flag icon.

If you swipe on a threaded message, the action you choose (Trash, Flag, Read, or Unread will apply to the whole of the thread).

Customize alerts

- Launch the **Apple Watch application on your iPhone.**
- Touch **My Watch, navigate to Mail > Custom, touch an account, then switch on Show Alerts from (name of the respective account).**
- Switch **Sound and Haptic either on or off.**

You can also be notified when an essential communication arrives while wearing your Apple Watch but not connected to your iPhone. Open the Apple Watch app on your iPhone, then touch My Watch, Mail, and then Email Notifications. When the iPhone is not connected

Shorten your message list

If you would like to make your mailing list a bit more compact, limit the number of preview text lines displayed for each email in the list.

- Launch the **Apple Watch application on your iPhone.**
- Touch **My Watch, touch Mail, and then touch Message Preview.**
- Make **a choice to show just 1 or 2 lines, or you can also choose not to show any lines.**

Load remote images

Some emails may contain links to web photos. When you enable remote photos to load, they display in the email.

To allow these photos, take the following steps:

- Launch the **Apple Watch application on your iPhone.**
- Touc**h My Watch, touch Mail, touch Custom**, and switch on **Load Remote Images.** It is worth noting that loading remote images can make the email download in a slower pattern on your Apple Watch,

Organize by thread

To have a view of all of the responses to an email altogether in a single thread, follow the steps below;

- Open the **Apple Watch application on your iPhone.**
- Touch **My Watch, choose Mail, pick Custom, and then switch on Organize By Thread.**

Change your email signature

Messages sent from your Apple Watch are signed with Sent from my Apple Watch by default. **To update it, take the following steps:**

- Launch the **Apple Watch application on your iPhone.**
- Choose **My Watch, touch Mail, and then choose Custom.**

- Touch the **Signature, then design a new signature.**

Activity

1. Check out the notification center on your watch and configure the various settings you need to your taste.
2. Request a call from a friend and attempt to pick up the call from your phone.
3. Send a message with the use of your Apple Watch.
4. Send an email with the use of your phone.

CHAPTER 5
HEALTH AND FITNESS MASTERY

Gaining health and fitness mastery is quite important for various reasons as it directly impacts diverse aspects of an individual's life. Good health and fitness help to contribute to an all-round physical well-being. Frequent exercise, a balanced diet, and proper rest can help with the prevention and effective management of chronic illnesses like heart disease, diabetes, and obesity. The Apple Watch is a very powerful tool that helps you gain mastery over your health and fitness. It provides a wide range of features and functionalities that are created to check, motivate, and also offer support to your health and fitness goals. In this section, you will learn about the various ways in which this amazing watch helps to ensure you are healthy.

Health and Fitness Overview

Health and fitness are only two of the numerous terms used to describe persons who are in good shape. There are several services and products available that promise to promote or maintain one's well-being, and any (or all) of these items and services may be considered to be part of the health and fitness business. These can encompass anything from medical services to sports, recreation, diet, and natural cures. There are also other methods for working with the body to improve physical fitness.

Calisthenics, jogging, and weight training were some of the earliest styles to gain popularity. Many additional types of exercise have evolved over time, including aerobics, yoga (which has been around for centuries), Pilates, and hybrids of each of these, such as yogalates, body pump, and water aerobics, among many others. Physical fitness is the ability of the heart, blood vessels, lungs, and muscles to work at peak efficiency - but fitness is much more than that! Another part of fitness is a person's mental attitude toward life. Mental stress (pressures from job, home, etc.) can have an impact on fitness just as much as hunger or physical damage. Physical fitness and stress are frequently linked.

Basic Components of Physical Fitness

Strength

Most individuals believe that being fit equates to being strong. In some ways, this is correct; yet, strength is not the only aspect of fitness. Strength is a muscle's ability to produce maximum force against resistance. Strength training (exercising to enhance strength) will cause muscle fiber expansion and a relative increase in your ability to apply force. Weight resistance programs (exercise with barbells, for example) are the most effective strategies to increase quick strength.

Flexibility

Flexibility refers to the capacity to use a muscle across its whole range of motion. It mainly refers to your ability to move your joints. A person who can touch their toes is far more adaptable than someone who cannot. Exercises that stretch muscles to their full extent, such as touching the toes, are the best approach to increase flexibility.

Motor Skill Performance

This is the nerves' ability to accept and send signals that result in smooth, coordinated muscle movement. This is demonstrated by your ability to dodge, maintain balance, respond and move fast, and so on. Vertical jumps, agility runs, squat thrusts, and other motor skill workouts are examples.

Cardiorespiratory Endurance

This relates to your hearts, blood vessels, and lungs' ability to distribute nutrients and oxygen throughout your body. Vigorous activity raises the need for oxygen in the cells. This implies you must take in more oxygen and your heart must pump more blood throughout your body. Vigorous exercise is the most effective way to improve cardiorespiratory endurance. But be cautious: too much too quickly can be harmful. The Apple Watch Series 9 is one of the most feature-rich smartwatches available. It counts steps and calories burnt, records sleep patterns, and tracks monthly cycles, but there are many additional health benefits to this sophisticated technology that you may not be aware of. It, for example, provides apps that examine heart rate patterns and electrical signals (ECG) for anomalies. It can also monitor your blood oxygen levels, which, if too low, can indicate respiratory or circulation problems.

Heart Health Monitoring: Insights and Trends

When something unusual happens, your Apple Watch can monitor your heart and notify you. For instance, your Apple Watch can alert you if, after at least 10 minutes of inactivity, your heart rate is still above or below a selected threshold. When you first launch the Heart Rate app, or at any point thereafter, you can enable heart rate notifications. If your Apple Watch detects a heart rhythm that seems to be atrial fibrillation (AFib), you can also get a notification. Your Apple Watch can help you determine how frequently your heart has AFib if you have already received a diagnosis. You can keep tabs on lifestyle elements that can affect your disease.

Check your heart rate on the Apple Watch

A key indicator of how your body is doing is your heart rate. You can take a reading at any moment, check your heart rate while exercising, and view your resting, walking, exercise, and post-workout heart rates, and your heart rate during a breathing session. Note: Ensure that your Apple Watch and wrist are both dry and clean. A bad recording can be a result of water and perspiration.

See your heart rate

Open the Heart Rate application on your Apple Watch to see your current heart rate, resting rate, and also your walking average rate.

See a graph of your heart rate data

- Launch the **Heart Rate application on your Apple Watch.**
- Switch the **Digital Crown to Current, Resting Heart Rate, or Walking Average to display your heart rate all through the day.**

Open the Health app on your iPhone, tap **Browse, press Heart, and then tap an entry to view your heart rate statistics over a longer period of time**. Heart data from the previous hour, day, week, month, or year can be displayed.

Receive high or low heart rate notifications

- Open the **Settings applications on your Apple Watch**, then touch **Heart.**
- Touch **High Heart Rate Notifications or Low Rate Notifications**, then configure **a heart rate threshold.**

You can also choose to open the Apple Watch application on your iPhone, touch My Watch, and then tap Heart. Touch High Heart Rate or Low Heart Rate, then configure a threshold.

Set up irregular heart rhythm notifications (not available in every region)

You can choose to receive a notification if the Apple Watch has recognized an irregular rhythm that seems to be atrial fibrillation (AFib).

- Open **the Apple Watch application on your iPhone.**
- Touch **My Watch, touch Heart, and then touch Set Up Irregular Rhythm Notifications in Health.**
- In the Health application, touch **Set Up**, then the **instructions on the screen.**

Show AFib history

- If you happen to have been diagnosed with AFib, launch the **Health application on your iPhone, then touch Browse.**
- Touch Heart, navigate down to Get More from Your Health, touch **Set Up beneath AFib History, and then proceed with the instructions on the screen.**
- To display your AFib history, launch the Health application, touch **Browse, touch Heart, and then touch AFib History.**

On Mondays, if you have worn your watch for at least 5 of 7 days (12 hours a day), you may receive a notification with an estimate of the time you spent in AFib during the previous calendar week.

Receive low cardio fitness notifications

By tracking how hard your heart is working while you walk, run, or hike outside, Apple Watch can estimate your level of aerobic fitness and notify you when it drops. Your level of aerobic fitness will fall into one of four categories, depending on your age and sex: Low, Below Average, Above Average, or High. You'll get a notification on your Apple Watch if your cardiac fitness level is in the "Low" area. Every four months, you'll be notified if it doesn't change.

- Open the **Settings application on your Apple Watch.**
- Touch **Heart, touch Cardio Fitness Notifications**. You can also choose to open the **Apple Watch application on your iPhone,** touch **My Watch, touch Heart, and then switch on Cardio Fitness Notifications.**

ECG and Blood Oxygen Monitoring

With only a few button taps, the Apple Watch can do a wide range of tasks, like taking an ECG and measuring blood oxygen levels. It can track and keep track of all the crucial data, including your daily activity and calorie expenditure as well as your ongoing heart rate, sleep, and other factors. You can perform an ECG (electrocardiogram) test on the Apple Watch to check for anomalies in your heart rhythm, often known as atrial fibrillation (Afib), which is another beneficial function for heart health.

Follow the steps below to make use of ECG on your Apple Watch;

- To start with, ensure that both your iPhone and Apple Watch are running the latest versions of their respective software. Since you are using the series 9, you should be more concerned about your phone. Go to Settings > General > Software Update on your iPhone to check.
- Go to the **Health app on your iPhone.**
- If you do not immediately get a prompt to configure the ECG application, locate **Browse > Heart > Electrocardiograms (ECG), and Set Up the ECH App.**
- Once the configuration has been completed, go to your **Watch, navigate to the text menu, and choose the ECG app**

- A notification will be displayed showing the New Classifications that are able to check for AFib.
- Read, move downwards, and choose **Done**.
- You will get a notice giving you a reminder that you should ensure that the Apple Watch is fitted snugly on the wrist you said it was on in Settings. If you changed to the opposite wrist, locate **Update Settings prior to taking an ECG** to get the most accurate measurement. If it is correct, choose **OK.**
- You will then see the image of a floating heart and you will get a prompt to hold your **finger on the Crown**. This oftentimes will be at the top, right side of your Watch.

- Hold your finger on the crown as instructed for about 30 seconds.
- You will see a readout of your Sinus Rhythm after 30 seconds of keeping your finger motionless, and it will indicate whether or not indicators of Afib were found. If so, you must always seek advice from a physician or other qualified healthcare provider.
- Navigate **down and Add Symptoms** if need be to get them saved to notes and then choose **Done**.

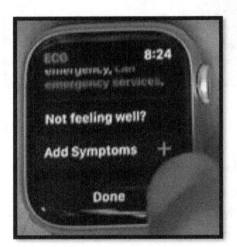

- If you get an inconclusive result, wait some minutes and take the test again.

There are five results you can get when taking an ECG from an Apple Watch.

- **Sinus rhythm**: this helps to confirm your heart is beating consistently at anywhere from 50 to 100 beats per minute (bpm).
- **Atrial fibrillation**: if you get this result, this means that your heart is beating in quite an irregular pattern, and should book an appointment with your doctor.
- **Low or high heart rate**: A low heart rate is considered to be one beneath 50 bpm, which can be caused by certain medications or if you are training to be an elite athlete. Also, a high heart rate could also be related to nervousness, alcohol, dehydration, infection, etc
- **Inconclusive**: This outcome indicates that the test was unable to identify your ECG, which could be the consequence of a pacemaker, symptoms of a heart problem the app cannot identify, or even a physiological condition that inhibits a signal

from creating a good recording. The best course of action is to wait around an hour and try again.

- **Poor recording:** Poor recording could be indicated by a reading. Make sure to rest your arm while taking the reading on a table or other flat surface to help avoid this. For the entire 30 seconds, take it easy and avoid making any sudden movements. As stated in Settings, make sure your wrist is dry and clean and that the Apple Watch is on the correct wrist. To prevent interference from other plugged-in equipment as well, look for a calm area.

Checking for blood oxygen on Apple Watch

As long as you have background measurements enabled, the Blood Oxygen app for Apple Watch measures your blood oxygen level throughout the day.

But you may manually take a measurement whenever you wish by doing so.

- Open the **Blood Oxygen application on your Apple Watch.**
- Place your arm on a table, your lap, or any other flat surface, and place the Watch face up. You will see diverse tips for taking a good measurement on screen. Touch **Next** until all of these are finished.
- Choose **Start.**
- A timer will commence counting from 15 seconds. Ensure you keep still all of the time.
- Your blood oxygen level will then appear as a percentage. Although some people can function with blood oxygen levels lower than 95%, a healthy blood oxygen level should be between 95 and 100%. To learn more, speak to your doctor. Click **Done.**
- You can also access the measurement after it has been taken by calling it up in the Health app's historical data. You may also view the data the Apple Watch collected throughout the day there.

Interestingly, you can use the Google Fit app on an iPhone to track your heart rate if you don't have a smartwatch. However, having access to 24/7 heart rate measurements and the ability to perform an ECG on demand is a terrific tool for anyone with cardiac issues to monitor their heart health. Although the smartwatch's ECG capability is not medically related and shouldn't be used to make diagnoses, it may identify potential problems and lead you to schedule a consultation with your doctor to talk about them. The app's capability to display previous readings is helpful for a medical expert to evaluate if anything seems off. The same is true for blood oxygen, which can be used to identify diseases like sleep apnea, probable cardiac or respiratory problems, or even to observe how drugs, blood pressure, coughing, and other factors may affect your blood oxygen level.

Advanced Workout Tracking and Analysis

There are various workouts that you can do and track with the use of the Apple Watch Series 9. It is no longer news that having a daily workout session helps to ensure you keep fit and also maintain being healthy. In this section, you will learn about the various workouts you can track with the use of the Apple Watch Series 9.

Walking

Make a choice of the Indoor walk for walking on a treadmill or for when you have to walk indoors like on an indoor track or in a mall. If you would like to improve the accuracy of pace and distance for Indoor Walk, at first there is a need for you to accumulate at least 20 minutes of outdoor walking with the use of the workout application to calibrate your watch. **Make a choice of Outdoor Walk for activities such as walking on a track or in the park. You may need to bring your iPhone along with you to track certain metrics;**

- **Pace and distance**: Apple Watch Series 9 has built-in GPS to track these metrics and also make provision for a map of your walk in the workout summary on your iPhone. When you have your iPhone with you, your watch then makes use of the GPS from your iPhone for the preservation of the battery. For a more accurate GPS hold your iPhone in your hand, or you can also choose to wear it on your armband or waistband. If there is a need for you to leave your iPhone behind, not to worry as you can still track the pace and distance of your workout with the use of the built-in accelerometer. If there is a need to have the accuracy of these metrics improved, bring your iPhone along with you first and accumulate a minimum of 20 minutes of door walking with the use of the Workout application for the calibration of your watch.

- **Elevation**: Your Apple Watch Series 9 has a built-in altimeter that can help with tracking this metric. You have no need to come along with your iPhone to track your elevation.

Running

Choose Indoor Run for running on a treadmill or any time that you have to run indoors. If you would like to improve the accuracy of pace and distance for Indoor Run, first you should accumulate at least 20 minutes of outdoor running with the use of the Workout app to calibrate your watch. You really have no need to come along with your iPhone. Make a choice of outdoor run for activities such as running on a track, trail, or road. With the use of the Apple Watch Series 9, you can make a choice of how you prepare for a long-distance run such as a marathon.

Below are some of the options worth considering;

- Low Power Mode helps to disable the Always On display and also reduces cellular data, GPS, and heart rate readings while walking and running or doing various workouts.
- You are able to synchronize music and podcasts straight to your Apple Watch before time so you are able to enjoy your content when you are not within the range of your iPhone.
- You can also choose to come along with your iPhone so that your watch can make use of Bluetooth for battery-intensive functions such as connectivity, streaming music or podcasts, gaining access to Siri, and lots more.
- If your long-distance run is much later in the day, you can keep your battery life by switching off cellular and the Always on display in the hours prior to your run.

Cycling

If you want to do things like ride a stationary bike or take a spin class, pick Indoor Cycle. If you want to ride a bicycle outside, pick Outdoor Cycle. You can choose to bring your iPhone along if you want to track specific metrics with your Apple Watch. For both indoor and outdoor workouts with watchOS 10, you may monitor your cadence (RPM), speed (MPH), and power (Watts) in your Workout monitor if your watch automatically connects to a Bluetooth-enabled cycling attachment that is compatible. A cycling session that you begin on your watch will also instantly appear as a Live Activity on your iPhone.

High-Intensity Interval Training (HIIT)

Select **HIIT for cycles of vigorous exercise**, followed by condensed rest or recovery intervals. You might, for instance, jump rope for 45 seconds, take a break for 30 and then repeat. A heart rate measurement may not be possible due to some of the erratic movements in HIIT exercises. Calories are still monitored using the onboard accelerometer if heart rate monitoring is not available. If your heart rate fluctuates when doing HIIT exercises, you can pair your Apple Watch with a Bluetooth chest strap.

Hiking

To keep track of your pace, distance, elevation gain, and calories burned, select hiking. During the workout, you may view your elevation increase in real-time, as well as your overall elevation gain. You can use the altimeter built into the Apple Watch Series 9 to determine and display your elevation while working out without needing to bring your iPhone.

Swimming

You have the option of swimming in a pool or open water with the Apple Watch Series 9. The screen automatically locks as the workout begins to stop water droplets from accidentally tapping it. You can check your training history, including auto sets and splits, and learn how to swim with your Apple Watch.

Below are ways in which Apple Watch helps to measure each workout;

- **Pool Swim**: When you commence a workout, ensure you accurately configure the pool length to aid your Apple Watch in measuring laps and distance. GPS isn't used during a Pool Swim and water may come in the way of a heart measurement, but calories, laps, and distance will still be tracked with the use of the built-in accelerometer.

- **Open Water Swim**: GPS will only offer distance when you get a freestyle stroke done. Water might prevent the measurement of heart rate but calories will still be measured with the use of the built-in accelerometer.

Wheelchair

If you are a manual wheelchair user, you have the option to make a choice of Outdoor Wheelchair Walk Pace or Outdoor Wheelchair Run Race. You ought to choose the one that completely describes your activity, but you do not have to keep a steady pace and you can also choose to have a mixture of speeds in either one. Making a choice of one for workouts done at or about a walking speed and the other workouts done at about a running speed will aid in keeping track of your workouts in the activity application.

Multisport

For Triathletes and Duathletes, the MultiSport workout type instantly switches between any sequence of swimming, cycling, and running workouts with the use of the motion sensors in your Apple Watch to check for various workout patterns. **You can choose to browse and include a new workout in the Workout application by following the set of instructions;**

- On your **Apple Watch, launch the Workout application**.
- Navigate **down** and touch **Add Workout.**
- Touch **the preferred workout.**

Make a choice of other when you are unable to locate a matching workout type. Through all workouts, the Heart Rate and Motion sensors work together to provide you with detailed credit. When you make use of other or any workout type that is available in the Add Workout section, you get a credit that is equal to a brisk walk when these sensor readings are not available.

Follow the steps below to commence working out with the use of your Apple Watch;

- Open the **Workout application.**
- Search for the workout that seems more like the best match to whatever you are doing.

- If you would like to create a goal, touch **the more button** close to the workout that you would like to do. You can also choose to create a custom workout. If also you would like to skip setting a goal, touch the workout.
- Pause **for the three-second countdown.** If you have a need to skip the countdown, touch the screen.
- To include another type of workout without putting an end to your current session, open the Workout application, then move to the right. Touch **End, then choose New Workout.**

End, pause, or lock your workout

- If you would like to put an end to your workout, move to the right, then touch the End button. Then touch **End Workout.**
- If you need to put a pause on a workout, swipe to the right side, then touch the Pause button. Or you can also choose to touch both the Digital Crown as well as the side button at the same time. When the need to pause is over and you would like to continue, touch both buttons once more.
- If you commence a swimming workout, your screen will lock instantly in order to prevent accidental taps from droplets of water. To unlock the screen, touch the **Digital Crown.**

Track your progress

If you would like to have a view of how well you are doing during a workout, raise your wrist. Turn the Digital Crown to have a view of another Workout.

Based on the workout being done, you can choose to include Workout views like;

- Heart Rate Zones
- Running Power
- Segments
- Splits
- Elevation
- Activity Rings

Whenever you either run, or walk, your Apple Watch touches every mile or kilometer, and it then displays an update on the screen. If you happen to be cycling, your Apple Watch taps you every five miles or kilometers.

Customize a workout

You can choose to include structured intervals in almost all workouts;

- On your Apple Watch, open the **Workout app.**
- Touch the More button close to the workout that you would like to embark upon.
- Move down and touch Create Workout, then touch **Custom.**
- Touch **Warmup to configure a Goal Type or Skip.**
- Touch **Add**, then touch **Work or Recovery, and choose a Goal Type.**
- Touch **Cooldown to configure a Goal Type or Skip.**
- Insert the **Custom Title of your Workout**, then choose **Done.**
- Touch **Create Workout.**

Your custom workout will then be displayed as an available goal option for the workout you have chosen. Metrics for your workout don't have to be the same over time, you can choose to alter the metric for each of workout.

Follow the steps below to get this done;

- On your Apple Watch, open the **Workout application.**
- Touch the **More button** close to the workout that you would like to embark upon.
- Navigate **down and touch Preferences.**
- Touch **Workout Views**, then touch the **Edit button close to the view.**
- Touch the **Edit button** close to the goal.
- Touch **Workout Views** and then touch **Edit Views.**
- Touch **Include** to add your preferred metric to your Workout View. You are also at liberty to touch the **Edit button close to a metric,** and then choose the metric you would like to edit.

Based on the actual type of workout, some of the metrics you can include are;

- Heart Rate

- Power
- Segments
- Splits
- Elevation
- Pace
- Cadence
- Distance
- Duration
- Vertical Oscillation
- Running Stride Length
- Ground Stride Length
- Ground Contact Time
- Speed
- Calories

Marking segments in your workout

To keep track of various portions of your workout, use segments. For instance, you may mark each lap or distance during an outdoor run session on a track. You may break up a 30-minute Indoor Cycle workout into three separate 10-minute sessions.

This is how:

- While the workout is ongoing, touch the screen twice.
- Pause for the summary of the segment to be displayed.

If you would like to have a view of all your segments after a workout, follow the steps below;

- Open the **Fitness application on your iPhone.**
- Touch **Show More beside History.**
- Touch the **Workout, then navigate downwards.**

You can't mark segments since your screen locks while you're swimming. However, in pool swim workouts, sets are automatically noted each time you take a 10-second or longer break at the pool's edge. In the exercise summary of the iPhone's Fitness app, Auto Sets are visible.

Get reminders to commence or end a workout

With watchOS 10, your Apple Watch will tap you on the wrist and prompt you when it detects that you are working out or have finished working out. To record, stop, or pause the workout, alter the type of workout, mute notifications for the day, or dismiss the notification, tap an option within the notification. No matter when you tap, you will only be given credit for the time spent working out. Your workout will continue if you ignore the notification or dismiss it until you decide to stop or pause. The period it takes for your watch to alert you to commence the recording or for you to put an end to a workout varies by the exact type of workout.

Below are some of the workouts that your watch can provide reminders for;

- Indoor Walk
- Outdoor Walk
- Indoor Run
- Outdoor Run
- Outdoor Cycling
- Elliptical
- Rower
- Pool Swim
- Open Water Swim

If you would like to turn off this configuration, launch the Settings application on your Apple Watch, touch Workout, and then navigate to Start Workout Reminder or End Workout Reminder.

Exploring Sleep Tracking and Stress Management

You may make sleep regimens using the Apple Watch's Sleep app to help you achieve your sleep objectives. Wear your watch to bed, and the Apple Watch can predict when you might have woken up as well as how much time you spend in each stage of sleep (REM, Core, and Deep). Open the Sleep app when you wake up to discover how much sleep you received and your sleep patterns over the previous 14 days. You are reminded to charge your Apple Watch if it is less than 30% charged before night. Simply take a quick look at the welcome in the morning to determine how much charge is left. Note: The Apple Watch does an amazing job of keeping track of your sleep depending on your sleep schedule (the one you must have created in the watch). Apple Watch also helps with the tracking of your sleep when your Sleep Focus commences. To get sleep data from the Apple Watch, it must first get your sleep tracked for a minimum of four hours per night. You can design various schedules; for instance, one for weekdays and another for weekends.

For each of the schedules, you can choose to configure the following;

- A sleep goal(this is simply the number of hours you would like to sleep for)
- What time do you want to go to bed and when do you want to wake up?
- An alarm sounds to get you up from the bed.
- When you would like to turn on the Sleep Focus, which reduces distractions prior to you going to bed and also helps to protect your sleep after you are already in bed.
- Sleep tracking, which makes use of your motion to detect sleep when you wear an Apple Watch to bed and the Sleep Focus is in use. It is worth noting that sleep tracking is available on the Apple Series Watch 9.

Set up Sleep on Apple Watch

- Launch the **Sleep application on your Apple Watch.**

- Proceed with the onscreen instructions. You can also make use of the open Health application on your iPhone, touch **Browse, touch Sleep**, and then choose **Get Started (beneath Set up Sleep).**

Change or turn off your next wake-up alarm

- Launch the **Sleep application on your Apple Watch.**
- Touch the **schedule icon.**
- If you would like to configure a new wake-up time, touch the wake-up time, switch the **Digital Crown to configure a new time, and then proceed.**

If you don't need your Apple Watch waking you up in the morning, you can choose to turn off the Alarm. You are also free to launch the Health application on your iPhone, touch **Browse,** touch **Sleep,** and then touch **Edit beneath** Your Schedule to alter your schedule. Note that these changes apply only to your next wake-up alarm, after which you will return to your normal schedule.

Change or add a sleep schedule

- Launch th**e Sleep application on your Apple Watch.**
- Touch the **alarm icon.**

- **Switch the Digital Crown to navigate down to Full Schedule, then do any of the following;**

    o **Alter a sleep schedule**: Touch **the current schedule.**

- o Include a sleep schedule: Touch **Add Schedule.**
- o **Change your sleep goal:** Touch your **Sleep Goal, then configure the amount of time you would like to sleep.**
- o **Change Wind Downtime:** Touch **Wind Down**, then configure the amount of time you would like the Sleep Focus to be active prior to bedtime. The Sleep Focus will then switch off the watch display and reduce distractions prior to your scheduled bedtime.
- **Commence any of the following;**
  - o **Configure the days for your schedule:** Touch your **schedule, then touch Active On. Make a choice of the days then touch the backward arrow.**
  - o **Adjust your wake time and bedtime:** Touch **your schedule, touch Wake Up or Bedtime**

- • **Turn the Digital Crown to configure a new time, and then proceed.**
- o **Set the alarm options:** Touch **the schedule, then switch the Alarm off or on and touch Sound & Haptics to make a choice of your alarm sound.**
- o **Remove or cancel a sleep schedule:** Touch y**our schedule, then touch Delete Schedule (at the lower part of the screen) to take off a schedule that exists, or touch the cancel icon to cancel and then create another one.**

Change sleep options

- Open the **Settings application on your Apple Watch.**
- Touch **Sleep**, then alter these settings;
    - **Turn On at Wind Down**: By default, the Sleep Focus commences at the wind-down time you configure in the Sleep app. If you would like to have control of the Sleep Focus manually in the Control Center, switch this option off.
    - **Sleep Screen**: Your Apple Watch display and iPhone Lock Screen are made simple in order to bring about a reduction in distraction.
    - **Show Time**: Display the date and time and iPhone and Apple Watch while the Sleep Focus is made active.
- Ensure Sleep Tracking and Charging Reminders are either turned on or off.

The Health app on your iPhone receives sleep data when Sleep Tracking is enabled on your Apple Watch. To have your Apple Watch remind you to charge it before bedtime and to let you know when it is fully charged, turn on Charging Reminders. On your iPhone, you can also modify these sleep settings. On your iPhone, open the Apple Watch app, select My Watch, and then select Sleep.

View your recent sleep history

Open the Sleep app on your Apple Watch to see how much sleep you got the previous night, how long you spent in each stage of sleep, and how much sleep you obtained on average over the previous 14 days. **Note:** Watch Series 9 supports information on different sleep stages. Open the Health app on your iPhone, select Browse, then select Sleep to view your iPhone's sleep history. Tap Show More Sleep Data to get more information, such as the average amount of time you spend in each stage of sleep.

Review your sleeping respiratory rate

You can gain more understanding of your general health by using your Apple Watch to track your breathing rate while you sleep.

Once you've worn your watch to bed, take these actions:

- Open the Health application on your iPhone, touch **Browse,** and then touch **Respiratory.**
- Touch **Respiratory Rate, then touch Show More Respiratory Rate Data**. The Sleep entry displays a wide range of your respiratory rate as you have slept.

Note: Respiratory Rate measurements are quite not intended for medical use.

Turn off respiratory rate measurements

- Open the **Settings application on your Apple Watch.**
- Navigate to **Privacy & Security > Health.**
- Touch the **Respiratory Rate**, then **switch off the Respiratory Rate.**

You can also launch the Apple Watch application on your iPhone, touch My Watch, touch Privacy, and then switch off Respiratory Rate.

Activity

1. What does Health and Fitness mean as explained in this book?
2. Configure the Health Monitoring application on your watch.
3. Configure your ECG and Blood Oxygen application on your application.
4. Check out the sleep tracking and stress management app on your watch.

CHAPTER 6

ENHANCING YOUR EXPERIENCE WITH APPLICATIONS

You can enhance your experience with applications on your Apple Watch to ensure the device is more useful and tailored in such a way that it meets your specific needs. The Apple Watch itself comes with a whole lot of useful applications that can ensure that you are never bored all through the day even if you are far away from your phone. You also can choose to download more applications from the App Store to ensure that you have all that you will ever need to ensure you have a fulfilling day and never get to miss out on anything. In this chapter, you will learn about some of the various built-in applications that you can make use of in your Apple Watch.

The Built-in App Extravaganza

In this section, you will learn about some of the very important built-in applications that can be of extreme importance to you right from the comfort of your wrist.

Audio Books

For lovers of books and audiobooks especially, Apple Watch can help to sync audiobooks from Apple Books. It is worth noting that Audiobooks from other sources cannot be synced to Apple Watch, it has to be from Apple Books.

- Launch the **Apple Watch application on your iPhone**.
- Touch **My Watch, then touch Audiobooks.**
- Touch **Add Audiobooks**, then choose **Audiobooks to include them on your Apple Watch.**

If you have quite some storage space, the whole contents of the Audiobooks you are listening to at the moment and also the one listed beneath Want to Read will be synced instantly to your Apple Watch. Five hours from each of the Audiobooks you have added will be downloaded to your Apple Watch once there is an available space for it.

Audiobooks synchronize to the Apple Watch anytime it is connected to a source of power.

You can make use of the Audiobooks application to play audiobooks from Apple Books directly on your Apple Watch.

- After you have connected to Bluetooth headphones or speakers, launch the **Audiobooks application on your Apple Watch.**
- When you are on the Listen Now screen, switch the **Digital Crown to navigate through the artwork.**
- Touch **an audiobook to play the book.**

Playing audiobooks from your library

You can stream audiobooks from your audiobook collection to your Apple Watch if it's close to your iPhone or connected to Wi-Fi or a cellular network (for Apple Watch models with cellular).

- Launch the **Audiobooks application on your Apple Watch.**
- From the **Listen Now Screen**, touch t**he back arrow,** choose **Library**, and then touch y**our preferred audiobook to play it.** Note that audiobooks purchased from Apple Books can be played by members of your Family Sharing group. On the audiobook screen, touch **My Family, then choose your preferred audiobook.**

You also can make use of Siri to play audiobooks. This can be done by playing an audiobook in your library.

Camera Remote

This application is one I find absolutely amazing. I am thrilled with the fact that I can control my phone to take pictures with the use of my watch. All you have to do is position your iPhone for a photo, or a video, then make use of your Apple Watch to take the picture or video from a distance. By default, there is a three-second delay prior to the shot being taken, offering you time to bring down your wrist and raise your face when you are in the shot. **Follow the steps below to take pictures with the use of your phone;**

- Open the **Camera Remote application on your Apple Watch**.

- Place your iPhone to frame the shot with the use of your Apple Watch as a viewfinder. To get a zoom, switch the Digital Crown. To adjust exposure, touch the key aspects of the shot in the preview image.
- To then proceed to take the shot, touch the Shutter button. The photo is then taken in Photos on your iPhone but you can also have it reviewed on your Apple Watch.

Not just pictures now, you can also record videos with the use of the same process;

- Launch **the Camera Remote application on your Apple Watch.**
- Place your iPhone to frame the shot with the use of your Apple Watch as a viewfinder. Switch the **Digital Crown to zoom in.**
- Touch and hold the **Shutter button to commence recording.**

- Let go of the **Shutter button** to put an end to recording.

Review your shots

Make use of the following actions to review the shots you have taken on your Apple Watch.

- **View a photo**: Touch the thumbnail in the lower left.
- **See other photos**: Move either left or right.
- **Zoom**: Switch the Digital Crown.
- **Pan**: Move on a zoomed picture.
- **Fill the screen:** Touch the photo twice.
- **Show or conceal the Close button and the shot count:** Touch the screen and when you are done, touch Close.

Compass

The Compass app displays your current position, elevation, and the direction your Apple Watch SE or Apple Watch Series 5 or later is facing. You can use Backtrack to retrace your steps, create Compass Waypoints, and then determine the distance and direction between them on Apple Watch SE and Apple Watch Series 6 and later, receive notifications when you've surpassed a certain elevation, see an estimate of the location where your Apple Watch last made a cellular connection or an SOS call, and more. It is worth noting that if you remove the Compass app from your iPhone, it will also be removed from your Apple Watch.

Choose a compass view

On the Apple Watch Series 9, the Compass application has five different views.

- When you open the Compass application initially, your bearing will be displayed in the middle of the watch face, with the waypoints being displayed in the inner ring.

- Switch **the Digital Crown** so you can have a view of a large compass arrow with your heading beneath.
- Switch **the Digital Crown up two screens** so you are able to have a view of your incline, elevation, and also the coordinates in the inner ring of the compass. Your

bearing is on the outer ring. Waypoints that are close are usually displayed in the middle.

- Proceed to **switch the Digital Crown** to display the location of the waypoints you designed and also the instantly designed waypoints that help to mark just where you have parked your car, and also estimate the last location where your watch or your iPhone could establish a cellular connection and also where Emergency SOS was last available.
- Each screen that displays the compass dial has an Elevation button at the lower part of the display. Touch **the elevation icon to display a 3D-like view** of your waypoint elevations that are in relation to your current elevation.

Browse waypoints

In Watch Series 9, you can find waypoints; the ones you have designed in the Compass applications, and also waypoints from guides in the Maps application.

- Launch the **Compass application on your Apple Watch.**
- Touch the **I icon** at the upper top left of your watch, then touch **Waypoints.**
- Choose **Compass Waypoints** to display the waypoints you have designed in the Compass application and also instantly produce waypoints like the location of your parked car and the last estimated locations where cellular connectivity and Emergency SOS were available.
- Touch **a guide like My Places** or a guide you have designed in the Maps application, to see those waypoints. To ensure that a guide's waypoints keep being displayed in the Compass application, touch the guide, then switch off Show Waypoints.

Add a bearing

- Launch the **Compass application on your Apple Watch.**
- Touch the **I icon, then touch Bearing.**
- Switch the **Digital Crown to the bearing**, then touch the correct mark symbol.
- If you would like to clear the bearing, touch the **I icon**, move down, and then touch **Clear Bearing**.

Red spinning radar screen

If a red spinning radar screen is displayed when you open the Compass application, this may be a result of any of the following;

- **Apple Watch may be in a poor magnetic environment**: Compass is usually affected by certain magnetic materials in some watch bands.
- **Location Services is turned off**: If you would like to switch location service either on or off, launch the Settings application on your Apple Watch, touch Privacy, and then touch Location Services.
- **Compass Calibration is disabled**: To turn Compass Calibration either on or off, launch the **Settings application on your iPhone**, locate **Privacy & Security**, and then touch **System Settings**.

Cellular waypoints, when they are present, indicate the most recent or closest approximate location at which your Apple Watch or iPhone made a cellular connection with your carrier. The most recent or closest approximate area where your Apple Watch or iPhone identified that a carrier's service might be available to place an emergency call is marked by emergency call waypoints when it's available. Call connectivity or waypoint availability may be impacted by your surroundings, the environment, and other variables. Depending on these circumstances, reconnecting may not be possible close to these waypoints. The cellular waypoints feature has a need for an iPhone making use of iOS 17. It is worth noting that Emergency call waypoints are only available in the U.S., Canada, and Australia.

Contacts

You may browse, edit, and share contacts from other devices that share the same Apple ID in the Contacts app. additionally, you can build up a contact card with your own information and create contacts.

See contacts on your Apple Watch

- Launch the **Contacts application on your Apple Watch**.
- Switch the **Digital Crown to navigate through your contacts**.

- Touch your preferred contact to see their picture, or navigate down to have a view of their details such as their email address, home address, work address, and more.

If you would like to display your contact card, touch your profile picture at the top right of your watch.

Create a contact

- Launch the **Contacts application on your Apple watch**.
- Touch the **add icon.**
- Insert **the name of the contact** and you can also choose to add the name of the company.
- Include a phone number, email, and residential address, and then touch the proceed icon.

Share, edit, block, or delete a contact

- Launch the **Contacts application on your Apple Watch**.
- Switch **the Digital Crown** to navigate through your contacts.
- Touch **a contact,** navigate down, and then do any of the following;
  - **Share a contac**t: Touch **the share icon at the lower right,** then choose a **sharing option you would like to use.**
  - **Edit a contact**: Touch **the pen icon**, then touch information to modify. You can choose to take off a field like address or email by touching Remove below the field.

- ○ **Block a contact**: Touch **Block Contact.**
- ○ **Delete a contact**: Touch **Delete Contact**.

Find People, Devices, and Items

Finding individuals who matter to you and letting them know where you are is easy with the Find Individuals app. You may easily find friends and family members on a map if they share their positions with you using an iPhone, iPad, or Apple Watch. You can configure notifications to notify you when family or friends depart from or arrive at specific areas. It is worth noting that Find People may not be available in all regions.

Add a friend

- Launch the **Find People application on your Apple Watch**.
- Navigate down, and then touch **Share My Location.**
- Touch the **Dictation**, **Contacts, or Keypad buttons** to make a choice of a friend.
- Make a choice of how long you would like to share your location; for an hour, until the end of the day, or indefinitely.

Your friend will then get a notification that you have shared your location with them. They can make a choice of also sharing their own location with you. After your friend has agreed to share his location with you, you will be able to see their location in a list or on a map in the Find My app on iPhone, iPad, and Mac, or the Find People app on Apple Watch. If you would like to put an end to sharing your location, touch the name of your friend on the Find People screen then touch Stop Sharing. If you would like to put an end to sharing location with everyone, launch the Settings application on your Apple Watch, locate Privacy & Security then choose Location Service, and switch off Share My Location.

Find out where your friends are

- Launch the **Find People** application on your Apple Watch to have a view of a list of your friends, with each friend's approximate location and distance from you. Switch the **Digital Crown** to have a view of more of your friends.
- Touch **a friend** so have a view of their location on a map and an approximate address.
- Tap **the back icon in the top-left corner** to go back to the list of your friends.

If your friend is sharing their location while wearing an Apple Watch with cellular service but isn't carrying their iPhone, their location will be tracked using their Apple Watch.

Notify a friend of your departure or arrival

- Open **the Find People application** on your Apple Watch.
- Touch **the friend you would like to show**, then touch **Notify**.
- Switch **on Notify on the following screen**, then choose to notify your friend when you leave your location or arrive at their own location.

Get a notification about the location of your friend

- Open the **Find People application** on your Apple Watch.
- Touch **your friend,** navigate down, and then touch **Notify Me.**
- Switch on **Notify Me,** then make a choice to be notified when your friend either arrives or leaves their location.

Get directions to a friend

- Launch the **Find People application** on your Apple Watch.
- Touch **your friend**, navigate down, and then touch **Directions** in order to open the Maps app.
- Touch **the route to receive step-by-step directions** from your location to the current location of your friend.

Contact a friend

- Launch **the Find People application on your Apple Watch.**
- Touch **your friend, navigate down, touch Contact, and then touch an email address or phone number.**

Walkie-Talkie

A fun and easy way to communicate with someone who owns an Apple Watch-compatible device is through a walkie-talkie. Press a button to speak, then release it to listen when you're ready to hear their response, just like you would with a genuine walkie-talkie. Both parties must be connected to a walkie-talkie, whether it be via cellular connectivity, Wi-Fi, or a Bluetooth connection to an iPhone. It is worth noting however that walkie-talkie is not available in all regions.

Invite a friend to use Walkie-Talkie

- Launch **the Walkie-Talkie application** on your Apple Watch for the first time.

- Navigate **through the list of contacts, then touch a name to send an invitation**.

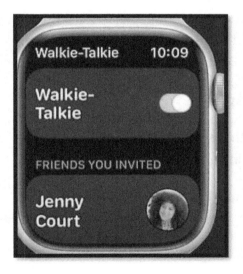

When your contact gets and accepts the invitation, you can commence a Walkie-Talkie conversation when the two of you are available. If you would like to include another contact, touch Add Friends on the Walkie-Talkie screen, then make a choice of a contact.

Have a Walkie-Talkie conversation

- Launch the **Walkie-Talkie application on your Apple Watch**.
- Touch **the name of your friend.**
- Touch and hold the **Talk button, then speak.**

If your friend has made themselves available, Walkie-Talkie opens on their Apple Watch and they will listen to what you said. If you also would like to modify the volume while you are talking, switch the Digital Crown.

Talk with a single tap

If you have problems with keeping your finger pressed on the Talk button, you can choose to make use of a single tap to talk.

- Open the **Settings application on your Apple Watch**.
- Touch **Accessibility, then underneath Walkie-Talkie, switch on Tap to Talk.**

Once this has been switched on, touch once to talk, then touch again when you are done talking. You can also choose to open the Apple Watch application on your iPhone, touch My Watch, touch Accessibility, then beneath Walkie-Talkie, and switch on Tap to Talk.

Apple Pay

On your Apple Watch, Apple Pay provides a quick, safe, and private payment method. You can use Apple Pay in the following ways with your cards connected to your Apple Watch and stored in the Wallet app on your iPhone:

- Shop in establishments that allow contactless payments and in applications that enable Apple Pay by using the credit, debit, and prepaid cards you add to the Wallet app.
- Payments between individuals: You can send and receive money quickly and securely through Messages or by using Siri.

If you unpair your Apple Watch or disable your passcode, you cannot use Apple Pay, and all cards you added to your Wallet are gone. If you disable your passcode, you must enter it each time you want to use Apple Pay.

Set up Apple Pay on the Apple Watch
Add a card to Apple with your iPhone

- Launch the **Apple Watch application on your phone.**
- Touch **My Watch, and then choose Wallet & Apple Pay.**

- If you have cards on your other Apple devices, or cards that you have just taken off, touch **Add** close to a card you would like to include

- Then insert the **CVV of the card**.
- For any other card, touch **Add Card**, then follow the instructions on the screen. Note that the issuer of your card may need more steps in order to have your identity verified.

Weather

Check the weather on the Apple Watch

With the use of the Weather application on your Apple Watch check current and upcoming weather conditions, locally or in locations around the world. You can with ease check on current weather details like clear or cloudy skies, temperature, precipitation, wind, ultraviolet (UV) conditions, visibility, humidity, and air quality. With the use of the weather application on your Apple Watch, you can see the following weather metrics; Current temperature, Conditions (mostly cloudy for instance), low and high temperatures for the day, Precipitation, Wind speed, UV index, Visibility, Humidity, Air quality. It is worth noting that Air quality readings are not available for every location. If local weather does not show on your Apple Watch when you launch the Weather app, ensure that Location Services is switched on. Launch the Settings application on your Apple Watch, touch Privacy & Security, and then switch on Location Services.

- On iPhone, locate **Settings > Privacy & Security > Location Services, touch Weather, then make a choice of your preferred option.**

Show weather forecasts

- Launch the **Weather application** from the Home screen on your Apple Watch.
- Navigate down one screen to display the forecast for the next 24 hours, which also includes conditions and temperatures.
- Move down one more screen to have a view of a 10-day forecast.

View individual weather metrics

You can display details about certain weather metrics like temperature, humidity, and air quality, and then display forecast information for that metric alone.

- **Choose a metric**: Touch **the weather icon** at the top right corner of the screen, then choose a metric like air quality. Switch the **Digital Crown** to display forecast information for that metric alone.
- **Cycle through metrics**: Touch **the display** to move through the metrics that are available.

See the weather in other locations on the Apple Watch

In addition to local weather, in the Weather application, you can display weather conditions and forecasts for locations you choose to include.

Add a location

- Launch the **Weather application on your Apple Watch.**

- Touch the **More or Options icon**, move to the lower part of the list of locations, then touch the **+ sign**.
- On supported Apple Watch models, type the name of the location, or make use of Scribble or dictation to insert the name of the location. To make use of Scribble on these same supported models, move up from the lower part of the screen, and then touch Scribble.
- Touch **Search**, then touch t**he location name in the list of results.**

The weather application on your iPhone displays the same locations, in the same order, that you include in the Weather application on your Apple Watch.

Remove a location

- Launch **the Weather application on your Apple Watch.**
- Touch the **More or Options icon, move to the left on the location you would like to remove, and then touch X.**

Choose your default location

- Launch the **Settings application on your Apple Watch.**
- Touch **Weather, touch Default City, and then make a choice from the list of various cities you included on your iPhone or Apple Watch.**

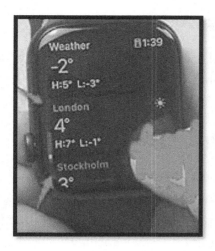

You can also launch the Apple Watch application on your iPhone, touch **My Watch, and then move to Weather > Default City.** Conditions for that specific location will be displayed on the watch face if you have had weather included with the face.

Workout

Get started with the Workout application on your Apple Watch

The Workout application on your Apple Watch offers you tools to manage your own workout sessions. You can choose to configure specific goals like time, distance, or calories. With the use of the Apple Watch, you can keep an eye on your progress, get a nudge as you work out, and summarize your results. You can make use of the Fitness application on your iPhone to check your complete workout history.

Choose a workout

The Workout app provides a range of training alternatives, from strength-based programs like Functional Strength Training, Core Training, and Kickboxing to cardio-focused routines like High-Intensity Interval Training (HIIT), Outdoor Runs, and Elliptical. Even sports-related exercises like baseball, basketball, and tennis can be started. Swipe down to the exercise you want to perform after launching the Workout app on your Apple Watch. Tap Add Workout if you can't find what you're looking for.

View metrics during a workout

Apple Watch shows stats like active calories, heart rate, and distance throughout a workout to help you track your progress. When working out, swipe left to see how you're doing.

Work out with gym equipment

You can get better information about your workout by pairing and syncing your Apple Watch with compatible cardio machines including treadmills, ellipticals, indoor bikes, and more. Simply place your Apple Watch close to the contactless reader on the exercise equipment, making sure that the display is facing the reader, and then press Start to get started.

Start a workout on the Apple Watch

- Open the **Workout application on your Apple Watch.**

- Switch **the Digital Crown to the workout** you would like to do. Touch **Add Workout** at the lower part of the screen for sessions like kickboxing or surfing.
- Anytime you are ready to go, touch **the workout.**

Pause and resume a workout

Press the side button and the Digital Crown simultaneously to pause the workout at any time. You may also slide right on the workout screen, then press **Pause**, for all workouts other than swimming workouts. Continue by **tapping Resume.**

Personalize workout views

Depending on the type of exercise you're doing, different workout perspectives will appear. By default, cardio-focused exercises offer more workout views, but you can change some of them to fit your training preferences.

- Launch **the Workout application on your Apple Watch.**
- Switch the **Digital Crown to the workout** you would like to do.
- Touch th**e more option, move down, then touch Preferences**.
- Touch **Workout Views.**
- Navigate through the workout views, then touch Include next to the metrics you would like to see during the workout.
- To choose the metrics that show in the first two workout views, touch the **pen icon in the Metrics or Metrics 2 set, choose a metric, and then choose another metric.**

End and review your workout on the Apple Watch

You experience a vibration and a tone upon reaching your objective. If you're feeling good and want to keep going, feel free to do so because your Apple Watch will keep gathering data until you tell it to stop.

When you're prepared to stop working out:

- Move **to the right, touch End, and then touch End Workout.**
- Switch **the Digital Crown** to navigate through the results summary, then touch **Done at the lower part of the screen.**

After a workout, the heart rate sensor continues to track your heart rate for three minutes. You may monitor your heart rate in real-time after an exercise by tapping the heart icon on your workout summary.

Organize Apps on the Apple Watch

You can arrange the applications on your Apple watch; in this section, you will get to know the various ways in which you can get this done.

Rearrange your apps in a grid view

- On your **Apple Watch,** touch the **Digital Crown to navigate to the Home Screen.** If the screen is in list view, move to the lower part of the screen, then touch Grid View.
- Touch and hold **an application**, then move the application to another location.

- Tap the **Digital Crown** when you are through.

Alternatively, you can tap My Watch, App View, and then Arrangement on your iPhone's Apple Watch app after opening it. Drag an app icon to a different location by **touching and holding it.** It is worth noting that in list view, applications are usually organized in alphabetical order.

Remove an application from your Apple Watch

For the app to be deleted from your Apple Watch, touch and hold the Home Screen and then tap the **X**. unless you also delete it on your linked iPhone, it stays there. In the list view, move to the left of the application, then touch the delete icon to take it off from your Apple Watch. If you take off an application from your iPhone, that application will also be deleted from your Apple Watch. If you have a need to restore an application that also includes a built-in Apple application, you can download it from the App Store on your iPhone or Apple Watch. It is worth noting that not all applications can be taken off from your Apple Watch.

Modify application settings

- Open the **Apple Watch application on your iPhone**.
- Touch **My Watch, then navigate down to have a view of the applications you installed.**
- Touch an application to alter its configurations.

The Apple Watch is also subject to some of the limits you've set for your **iPhone under Settings > Screen Time > Content & Privacy limits**. For instance, the Camera Remote icon is gone from the Apple Watch Home Screen if the Camera feature on your iPhone is off.

Check storage used by applications

On your Apple Watch, you can see how much storage is being utilized, how much is still available, and how much storage each app consumes.

- Launch **the Settings application on your Apple Watch.**
- Navigate to **General > Storage.**

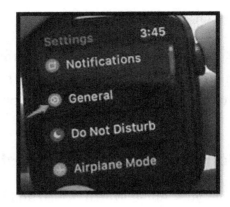

You can also choose to open the Apple Watch application on your iPhone, touch **My Watch, and then go to General > Storage.**

Tapping into the App Store

You may use the apps on your Apple Watch to keep track of time, keep track of your health, and communicate with others. Additionally, you have the option of installing any third-party apps you already own for your iPhone and downloading brand-new apps from the App Store from either your iPhone or Apple Watch. One Home Screen contains all of your installed apps. **Note:** Open the Settings app on your Apple Watch, hit the App Store, and enable Automatic Downloads to have the companion iOS version of an app you've installed to your Apple Watch downloaded automatically. Aside from turning on Automatic Updates, make sure your Apple Watch apps are updated so you may use the most recent versions.

Get applications from the App Store on Apple Watch

- Open the **App Store application on your Apple Watch**.
- Switch the **Digital Crown to browse feature applications and collections.**
- Touch **a collection** to have a view of more applications.
- If you would like to get a free app, touch **Get; to buy an app, touch the price.**

Tap the search icon in the upper left corner of the screen, then type (on supported models only; not available in all languages), utilize Scribble, or dictate the name of the app to search for it. By selecting a category, you can also browse popular app categories. If you would like to make use of Scribble on these same supported models, move up from the lower part of the screen, then touch Scribble. It is worth noting that when making use of Apple Watch with cellular, cellular data charges may be applied. Note also that Scribble is not available in all languages.

Install applications you already have on your iPhone

On your iPhone, watchOS apps that are available by default are downloaded and placed on the Home Screen. **Instead, take the following actions to select and install particular apps:**

- Launch the **Apple Watch application on your iPhone.**
- Touch **My Watch, touch General, and then switch off Automatic App install.**
- Touch **My Watch, then navigate down to the list of Available applications.**
- Touch **Install close to the applications you would like to install.**

Customizing Glances and Dock

The Apple Watch is a fantastic gadget with a host of features and capabilities that meld into our daily lives. The Apple Watch's Dock, a handy location to access your most frequently used apps, is one of its essential features. Did you know that you can change the Apple Watch Dock's default setting to show only your favorite apps instead of just a selection of recently used ones? The ability to rapidly access the apps that are most important to you, whether they are for fitness monitoring, communication, productivity, or entertainment, can significantly improve your Apple Watch experience. You'll be able to customize your Apple Watch Dock with your preferred apps and take advantage of a more tailored and effective Apple Watch experience.

Accessing the Dock on your Apple Watch

There are two major ways to gain access to the Dock on your Apple Watch;

- **Choosing the side button**: On your Apple Watch, tap the side button to open the Dock. This is the fastest way to gain access to the applications you like the most.
- **Using the Dock complication on a watch face**: If you have a Dock complication added to your watch face, you can touch it to get the Dock opened.

Adding Apps to Your Apple Watch Dock

Once you have gained access to the Dock; you can commence the addition of your preferred application. **There are basically two methods to get this done;**

- **Making use of the Apple Watch application on your iPhone**: Open the Apple Watch application on your iPhone and locate My Watch, Navigate to locate the Dock section, and then touch Edit close to Favorites, and you can choose and add applications of your choice to your Dock.
- **Customizing from your Apple Watch**: You can also choose to customize your Dock straight from your Apple Watch. In the Dock, navigate to the bottom and touch Edit. Then, you can proceed to add applications by touching the + icon.

Rearranging Apps in your Apple Watch Dock

If you have a need to rearrange the order of applications in your Apple Watch Dock, there are two different options you can choose to make use of;

- **With the use of the Watch app on your iPhone**: Launch the Apple Watch application on your iPhone and locate the **My Watch tab**. Navigate down to **locate the Dock section, then touch Edit close to favorites.** Tap and hold the three horizontal lines close to an application and then move it to the preferred position.
- **Rearranging your Apple Watch**: In the Dock, move up on an application and hold on to it until it gets to the editing mode. You can then move the application to another position by making use of the finger on the screen.

Removing Apps from your Apple Watch Dock

If you would like to remove an application from your Apple Watch Dock, follow the steps below;

- **Making use of the Apple Watch application on your iPhone**: Launch the Apple Watch application on your iPhone and locate My Watch. Move down to locate the **Dock section and then touch Edit close to Favorites**. Touch the red icon close to the application you would like to take off

- **Removing from your Apple Watch**: In the Dock, move up on an application and touch **the "-" icon** that shows close to it. Make a confirmation of the removal by touching on Remove in the window that pops up.

By customizing your Apple Watch Dock, you may locate your most often-used apps just a swipe away. By doing this, you may locate the program you need quickly and without having to search through numerous screens. Having your favorite apps conveniently located in the Dock enables seamless multitasking. You can easily switch between apps without interfering with your productivity, whether you need to send a quick message, check your fitness statistics, or manage your smart home devices. Making the Dock your own enhances the functionality of your Apple Watch while also reflecting your design and personal preferences. The apps can be customized to your needs so that the ones you value the most are always available.

Mastering Multitasking on a Tiny Screen

Don't mind the fact that your Apple Watch screen is quite small, you are able to multitask on the screen with the use of the App Switcher. With the use of the App Switcher, you can see your most recently used application, or switch from one application to the other.

Open an app from the App Switcher

- Tap **the side button.**
- Move either up or down, or you can also choose to switch **the Digital Crown.**
- Touch **an application to launch it.**
- To close the **App Switcher, tap the side button.**

Remove an app from the App Switcher

- Touch **the side button to open the App Switcher.**
- Go to any application, then move **to the left side.**
- Touch the **red x icon to remove the button.**

Sort by Recents or Favorites

The Dock can display your most recent applications or up to 10 of your favorite applications. When you touch **Recents**, your applications will show in the order that you have opened them. When you pick Favorites, you can pick the applications that show, but the app you recently used the most will still be displayed at the top of the Dock. If it's not already a favorite, you can touch Keep in Dock to include it. **Below are the steps to select what is displayed;**

- Launch the **Watch application on your iPhone.**
- Touch the **My Watch tab, then choose Dock.**
- Touch **Recents or Favorites.**

Add your favorite applications

If you organize the Dock by Favorites, you can make a choice of the applications to display or take off;

- **Launch the Watch application on your iPhone.**
- Touch the **My Watch tab, then choose Dock.**
- Ensure that Favorites is chosen.
- Choose **Edit**
  - o If you would like to remove an application, touch the remove button, then choose Remove.
  - o If you would like to include an application, touch the add button. You can include up to about 10 applications.
  - o If you would like to reorganize the applications, touch and hold **the reorder button** close to an application, then move either up or down.
    - To keep your changes, touch Done.

Activity

1. Check out the various in-built applications on your phone. Follow the explanation in this guide to have an idea of what they do.
2. Explore the App Store on your watch and consider some applications you might like to download.
3. Customize Glances in your watch.
4. Make use of the App switcher in multitasking on your phone.

CHAPTER 7
MUSIC, MEDIA, AND BEYOND

Playing Tunes: Local and Streaming

You can listen to music you've added to your Apple Watch wherever you are, even if your iPhone isn't nearby. Using the Apple Watch app on your iPhone, you can choose which albums and playlists to add to your Apple Watch. If you have Apple songs, you can also add songs to your Apple Watch via the Music app. If you have an Apple Music subscription, you do not need to select a specific piece of music to add to your Apple Watch. The most recent music you listened to is automatically added. (If you haven't listened to anything, Apple Music's suggestions are included.)

Note that if you are an Apple Music Voice subscriber, you can include music you have bought on your Apple Watch. If you would like to add songs, albums, and playlists from Apple Music, ensure you upgrade to a full Apple Music subscription.

Add music with the use of your iPhone

- Launch the **Apple Watch on your iPhone.**
- Touch **My Watch, then touch Music.**
- Beneath **Playlists & Album, touch Add Music.**
- Move to albums and playlists you would like to get synchronized to your Apple Watch, then touch the + icon to include them in the playlists and album queue.

Note that music is added when your Apple Watch is close to your iPhone.

Add music with the use of your Apple Watch

If you are a subscriber of Apple Music, you can choose to include music with the use of your Apple Watch. It is worth noting that adding music is not available in the Apple Music Voice plan.

- Launch **the Music application on your Apple Watch.**

- On the Listen Now Screen, locate **the music you would like to add. You can also touch the back arrow icon, touch Search, and then look for the music you would like to add.**
- Touch **a playlist or album, touch the three dots, then choose Add to Library**. A message confirming that the music has been added will be displayed.

It is worth noting that you can stream music you include on the Apple Watch when you have a connection to the internet. If you like to play music when you are not connected to the internet, there is a need for you to download it first.

- To download the music to Apple Watch, touch the **three dots** once more, then touch **Download**. It is worth noting that downloading music when your Apple Watch is not connected to power uses more of its charge than normal.

Add a workout playlist to Apple Watch

In the Workout app for Apple Watch, you can add a playlist from your music collection that starts playing as you begin a workout.

- Launch the **Apple Watch application on your iPhone.**
- Touch **My Watch, then touch Workout.**

- Touch **Workout Playlist**, then make **a choice of your preferred playlist.**

The playlist will then be added to **My Watch > Music** in the Apple Watch application on your iPhone. It is worth noting that a playlist will not play if you are currently listening to other music or audio.

Remove music from Apple Watch

Remove music that was added automatically to your Apple Watch or music that you no longer listen to if you're running out of space to keep audio on your watch.

Note: Open the Settings app on your Apple Watch, then select **General > Storage to view the amount of music that is saved there**. On your iPhone, open the **Apple Watch app, select My Watch, and then select General > Storage.**

Remove music with the use of your Apple Watch

If you have Apple Music, you can delete any music that has been added to your Apple Watch, whether it was done so voluntarily or automatically.

- Launch **the Music application on your Apple Watch.**
- From the Listen Now screen, touch **the back arrow icon, navigate down, touch Downloaded, and then choose Playlists or Albums.**
- Touch **a playlist or an album, touch the more options (three dots), and then touch Remove.**
- Choose a preferred option
  - **Remove Downloads**: This option removes the downloaded playlist or album from your watch. It will still be in your library hence you will be able to download it once more or stream it over Wi-Fi or cellular.
  - **Delete from the library**: with this option, the music will be removed from your Apple Watch and from every other device that uses the same Apple ID.

It is worth noting that you can also choose to delete single songs from your library. Move left on a song, touch the **more option, touch Delete from Library, then touch Delete**. The song will then be removed from your watch, from any playlists it's in, and also from all other devices that make use of the same Apple ID.

Play music on Apple Watch

To select and play music on Apple Watch, use the Music app. If you're a subscriber, you can stream music from Apple Music and Apple Music Voice, play music from your iPhone, and manage music on your Apple Watch.**You should note that not all features can be found in the Apple Music Voice Plan.**

- **Play music from your music library**: From the listen now screen, touch **the back arrow icon, touch the library, touch a category like a playlist, album, downloaded, or recently added item, then touch music.**
- **Play music on your Apple Watch**: Switch the **Digital Crown to navigate through the Listen Now screen, and then touch an album, playlist, or category.**

Play music for you

If you are an Apple Music subscriber, you can choose to play music chosen just for you.

- Launch **the Music app on your Apple Watch.**
- Navigate to **see the music you have just added to your Apple Watch** and a curated feed of playlists and albums depending on your likes and dislikes.
- Touch **your preferred category, album, or playlist, and then touch the play button.**

Play music on a different device

Not only can you stream music to a set of linked headphones from your Apple Watch, but you can also do this with other Bluetooth-enabled speakers and headphones. Additionally, you can manage the music on AirPlay-capable gadgets like the Apple TV and HomePod speakers. **On the Now Playing screen, choose the More option at the top right of the screen, and then get any of the following done;**

- **Connect to a Bluetooth device**: Touch **AirPlay, touch Choose a Device, then make a choice of a Bluetooth device.**

- **Connect to an Airplay device:** Touch **Airplay, touch Control Other Speakers TVs,** **then make a choice of a device, and then choose the music you would like to** **play.**

Listening to the radio on the Apple Watch

Apple Music 1, Apple Music Hits, and Apple Music Country are three Apple Music stations that can be found in the Radio section of the Music app on the Apple Watch. These stations offer the newest music in a range of genres as well as exclusive interviews. You can also listen to highlighted stations created by music professionals and broadcast radio. No subscription is needed for you to listen to Apple Music 1, Apple Music Hits, or Apple Music Country. Make sure your Apple Watch is close to your iPhone or connected to Wi-Fi or, if you have an Apple Watch with cellular, a cellular network, in order to listen to Apple Music radio.

- Launch **the Music application on your Apple Watch.**
- From the Listen Now Screen, touch **the right arrow icon, touch Radio, and then** **touch Apple Music 1, Apple Music Hits, or Apple Music Country.**

Listen to a featured or genre station

- Launch the **Music app on your Apple Watch.**
- From the **Listen Now Screen, touch the back arrow icon, touch Radio, and then** **switch the Digital Crown to move through stations and genres designed by music** **experts.**
- Touch **a genre** to have a view of its stations, then touch **a station** to have it played.

Explore radio stations

You can share songs and radio stations, add songs to your library or playlists, mark songs **you like and don't like, and access an artist or album screen while listening to a radio** **station.**

- Launch the **Music application on your Apple Watch.**
- Touch **the Radio,** then t**ouch a station to play it.**
- Touch the **three dots, and then choose your preferred option.**

Listen to broadcast radio

You can choose to listen to lots of broadcast radio stations on your Apple Watch. You can make a choice to ask for stations by name, call sign, frequency, and nickname. It is worth noting that you have no need for a subscription to Apple Music for you to listen to broadcast radio. Broadcast radio cannot be found in all countries or regions. Not all stations are available in all countries or regions.

Podcasts and Audiobooks on the Go

You can listen to podcasts on your Apple Watch even if your iPhone isn't with you by adding them to your watch. Using the Apple Watch app on your iPhone, you can add podcast episodes to your Apple Watch, or you may add them straight from your Apple Watch.

Add podcasts using your iPhone

Recent episodes of the shows you follow and create stations for on your iPhone's Podcasts app are accessible to download to your Apple Watch when it's plugged in.

- Launch **the Apple Watch application on your iPhone.**
- Touch **My Watch, touch Podcasts, then do any of the following;**
  - **Add episodes from stations**: Beneath Add Episodes From, touch Up Next, Saved, or a station, then make a choice of the number of episodes to download to your Apple Watch.
  - **Add episodes from podcasts you follow**: Below Shows, touch **Add Shows**, touch the **+ icon** close to the shows you would like to include, then touch Done.

When your Apple Watch is plugged into power, three episodes of each show are automatically added to the device. Tap a show, then select the desired number of episodes to adjust the number of episodes.

Follow and unfollow podcasts with the use of your Apple Watch

You can follow podcasts directly from your Apple Watch;

- Launch **the Podcasts application on your Apple Watch**.
- Do any of the options below;
    - On the Listen Now screen, touch **You Might Like or another category, touch your preferred show, and then touch the + icon.**
    - From the Listen Now screen, touch **the back icon, touch Search, insert the name of a podcast, touch the show you would like to follow, and then touch the + icon.**
- Touch **the More option button, touch Automatically Download, and then make a choice of a number of episodes to download** when your Watch is connected to a source of power.

If you would like to unfollow a show, touch Library, touch the show, touch the More option, then choose Unfollow Show.

See downloaded podcasts

- Launch **the podcasts application on your Apple Watch.**
- Touch **the More option**, choose **Library, and then touch Download.**

Play podcasts on Apple Watch

- After you have connected your Apple Watch to Bluetooth headphones or speakers, launch the podcasts application on your Apple Watch.
- **Do any of the following;**
    - Switch the **Digital Crown** to navigate through the Listen Now screen, then choose **a podcast or category**.
    - From the Listen Now screen, touch the back icon, choose **Library, touch Download, and then choose a podcast to play**.

Stream podcasts to your Apple Watch

You can stream podcasts to your Apple Watch if it's close to your iPhone and connected to Wi-Fi or a cellular network (for Apple Watch models with cellular).

Launch the Podcasts application on your Apple Watch, then get any of the following done;

- **Stream a suggested podcast library**: From the Listen Now screen, navigate down, touch your preferred category like More to Discover, and then touch an episode you want.
- **Stream from your podcast library**: From the Listen Now screen, touch the back icon, choose Library, and touch a show you would like to stream, touch the play icon in order to play the most recent episode, or navigate down, and then touch an older episode.
- **Look for a podcast to stream**: From the Listen Now screen, touch the back icon, choose Search, insert the name of a podcast, touch Search, touch a result, and then choose your preferred episode.

Change Podcasts settings

You can alter the Podcasts settings straight from your Watch.

- Launch **the Settings application on your Apple Watch.**
- Touch **Podcasts,** where you will be able to modify these settings;
- **Up Next:** Make a choice of the number of episodes downloaded to your Apple Watch from Up Next when your Apple Watch is being synced.
- **Saved**: Make a choice of the number of episodes not downloaded from Saved when your Apple watch is being synced.
- **Continuous Playback**: Switch on to play another episode after the current episode has ended.
- **Skip buttons**: Make a choice of the time interval used when touching the Skip Forward or Skip Back buttons.
- **External Controls:** Touch Next/Previous or Forward/Back to pick the behavior of headphone controls.
- **Reset Identifier:** Reset the identifier used for the reporting of aggregate application usage statistics to Apple.

AudioBooks

Add audiobooks to Apple Watch

Apple Watch can help with syncing audiobooks from Apple Books. It is worth noting that audiobooks from other sources cannot be synced to Apple Watch.

- Launch the **Apple Watch application on your iPhone.**
- Touch **My Watch, and then choose Audiobooks.**
- Touch **Add Audiobook, then make a choice of audiobooks to include on your Apple Watch.**

The complete contents of the audiobook you're now listening to, as well as the one noted under Want to Read, are instantly synced to your Apple Watch if there is enough storage space for both. When there is room available, five hours from each audiobook you upload is also downloaded to your Apple Watch. When connected to electricity, the Apple Watch syncs audiobooks.

Play audiobooks on Apple Watch

You can make use of the Audiobooks application to play audiobooks from Apple Books on your Apple Watch.

Play audiobooks saved on Apple Watch

- Once you have connected to Bluetooth headphones or speakers, launch **the Audiobooks application on your Apple Watch.**
- On the Listen Now screen, switch the **Digital Crown to navigate through the artwork.**
- Touch **an audiobook to play it.**

Play audiobooks from your library

You can stream audiobooks from your audiobook collection to your Apple Watch if it's close to your iPhone and connected to Wi-Fi or a cellular network (for Apple Watch models with cellular).

- Launch t**he Audiobooks application on your Apple Watch.**

- From the Listen Now screen, touch **the back icon, then touch Library, and then touch an audiobook to play it.**

You can also listen to audiobooks that members of your Family Sharing group have purchased from Apple Books. Tap My Family, then a book, on the Audiobooks screen.

Media Remote Control: iPhone, TV, and More

You can make use of the Remote application on your Apple Watch to play music on a computer that is on the same Wi-Fi network.

Add a music library

- Launch the **Remote application on your Apple Watch.**
- Touch **the + sign.**
  - If you are making use of the Music application on a Mac with the Mac 10.15 or later: Launch **Apple Music** and choose your **Apple Watch from the list of devices that is displayed in your library.**
  - If you are making use of iTunes on your Mac or PC: choose **the Remote button close to the top left of the iTunes window.**
- Insert **the 4-digit code shown on your Apple Watch.**

Control playback from Apple Watch

Do any of the following;

- Make **use of the playback controls in the Remote application.**
- Switch **the Digital Crown to modify the volume.**
- Make **a choice of an Airplay device.**

Choose a media library to play from

- **If you added more than just one library**: Touch **the one you prefer** when you open the Remote application on your Apple Watch.
- **If you are already playing music:** Touch **the back icon** at the top left of the playback, then touch **the library.**

Remove a media library

- Launch the **Remote application on your Apple Watch.**
- Move left on a library, and then touch **X to take it off.**

Control Apple TV with Apple Watch

You can choose to also make use of your Apple Watch as a remote control for your Apple TV when the TV and the watch are both on the same Wi-Fi network.

Pair your Apple Watch with Apple TV

If your iPhone has never connected to the Wi-Fi network that the Apple TV is connected to, do so right now. Then, proceed as follows:

- Launch **the Remote application on your Apple Watch.**
- Touch **your Apple TV.** If you are unable to find it in the list, touch the **+ icon.**
- On the Apple TV, locate Settings, Remote and Devices > Remote App and Devices, then choose Apple Watch.
- Insert **the passcode shown on your Apple Watch.**

When the pairing icon is displayed close to the Apple Watch, it is then ready to control the Apple TV.

Use your Apple Watch to control your Apple TV

Ensure the Apple TV is on, then follow the following steps;

- Launch **the Remote application on your Apple Watch.**
- Pick your **Apple TV,** then **move up, down, left, or right** to navigate through the Apple TV menu options.
- Touch to make a choice of the chosen item.
- Touch the **Play/Pause button to pause or resume playback.**
- Touch the **back arrow icon** to go back to the main menu.

You can also launch the Remote application from the Now Playing application. In Now Playing, touch the back arrow symbol, choose your **Apple TV,** touch the more options, and then touch **TV Remote**

Setting Up Bluetooth Devices and Audio Routes

You now can play audio from your Apple Watch on Bluetooth headphones or speakers without your iPhone close to you. If you have AirPods that you configure with the use of your iPhone, they are ready to be used with your Apple Watch; all you have to do is press play.

Pair Bluetooth headphones or speakers

The majority of Apple Watch audio must be listened to using Bluetooth headphones or speakers (Siri, phone calls, voicemail, and voice notes are played through the Apple Watch speaker). Put the speakers or headphones in exploration mode by following the directions that came with them. When the Bluetooth device is ready, carry out the following actions:

- Launch **the Settings application** on your Apple Watch, then choose **Bluetooth.**

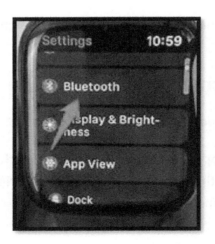

- Touch the device when it is displayed.

You can also choose to open the Bluetooth settings when you are on the screen of the Audiobooks, Music, Now Playing, and Podcasts.

Choose an audio output

- Touch the side button to open the Control Center.
- Choose the device you would like to make use of.

Monitor and adjust your headphone volume

- Tap the side button to launch the Control Center.
- While listening to your headphones, touch the ear symbol. A meter will then be displayed showing the current headphone volume.
- Touch the volume controls beneath Headphone Volume or touch the slider, then switch the Digital Crown to modify it.

Reduce loud sounds

Apple Watch can reduce how loud your headphone audio is in order to configure the decibel level.

- Launch the Settings application on your Apple Watch.
- Locate Sounds & Haptics

Headphone Safety

- **Then touch Reduce Loud Sounds.**
- Switch on **Reduce Loud Sounds, then configure a level.**

View loud headphone audio notifications

Apple Watch notifies you when you are wearing headphones and automatically lowers the volume to a more manageable level to preserve your hearing if you are listening to loud audio for an extended period of time.

If you would like to have a view about details as regards headphone notifications, follow the steps below;

- Launch the **Settings application on your Apple Watch.**
- Locate **Sounds & Haptics > Headphone Safety, and then touch Last 6 Months below Headphone Notifications.**

You can also launch the Health application on your iPhone, **touch Browse, choose Hearing, select Headphone Notifications, and then touch your preferred notification.**

Activity

1. Play music on your Apple Watch.
2. Play your preferred podcasts and audiobooks on your watch.
3. Control your iPhone with the use of your watch.
4. Configure your Bluetooth device and audio routes

CHAPTER 8

PRODUCTIVITY AND ORGANIZATION

Syncing Calendars and Using Organization

Your Apple Watch's Calendar app displays events you have scheduled or been invited to for the previous six weeks as well as the following two years (in List and Day view). Events from all of your iPhone's calendars or simply the calendars you select are displayed on your Apple Watch.

Viewing calendar events on Apple Watch

- Launch **the Calendar application on your Apple Watch**, or you can also choose to select **the date or a calendar event on the watch face.**

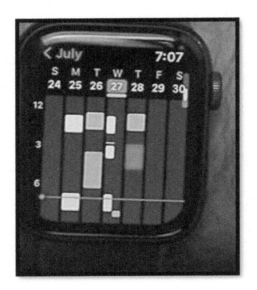

- Switch **the Digital Crown to navigate through events that are coming up**
- Touch **your preferred event to have a view of details about it which includes time, location, invitee status, and notes.**

If you would like to go back to the next event, touch the back icon in the top-left corner. You can also choose between seeing your events weekly or monthly.

Change how you view events

If you would like to change views, launch the Calendar application on your Apple Watch, touch the three dots, and then choose your preferred option.

- **Up Next:** displays your upcoming events for the week.
- **List**: displays all your events from the last two weeks through the next two years.
- **Day, Week, or Month:** displays events for the given period of time.

Swipe left or right in Day view to see another day; turn the Digital Crown in List view or Up Next view to see another day. Tap the time that is displayed in the top-right corner of the screen to return to the current day and time.

View weeks and months from the Day or List view

You can switch between week and month views while perusing events in the Day or List view.

Choose one of the following actions after opening the Calendar app on your Apple Watch:

- **Show the current week:** Touch **the back symbol in the top-left corner.**
- **Show a different week**: Move **left or right.**
- **Show events in a particular week:** Touch **a day on the weekly calendar.**
- **Show the current month:** While the current week is being displayed, touch **the back icon in the top-left corner.**
- **Show a different month:** Switch t**he Digital Crown.**
- **Choose a week in the monthly calendar:** Touch **the week.**

Add an event

Events you add to the iPhone's Calendar app are automatically synced with your Apple Watch. Events can also be created directly from your watch.

- **Make use of Siri:** Say something like "Create **a calendar event".**

151

- **Make use of the calendar application on Apple Watch**: When you are seeing events in the Up Next, Day, or List view, touch **the More option**, then choose **the + symbo**l.

Include event details like title, location, date and time, invitees, and make a choice of the calendar you would like to add the event to.

Delete or change an event

- **Delete an event you created**: Touch a**n event, choose Delete, and then choose Delete again.** If this is an event that reoccurs, you can choose to delete this event alone or all future events
- **Change an event**: Touch **an event, choose Edit, ensure you make your changes, and then proceed.**

Respond to a calendar invitation

You can reply on your Apple Watch to various event invitations when you get them or much later.

- **If you see the invitation when it arrives**: Navigate t**o the lower part of the notification, then pick Accept, Decline, or Maybe.**

- **If you discover the notification later**: Touch **it on your list of notifications, and then navigate and give a reply.**
- **If you are already in the Calendar app**: Touch **the event to reply.**

Hit the name of the event organizer in the event details, then hit the message or phone button, to get in touch with them. For more choices, tap the **More Options button**. You can also choose an alternative from the details on their contact card by swiping down to the next screen.

Get directions to an event

If an event has a specific location, your Apple Watch can give directions to it.

- Launch the **Calendar application on your Apple Watch.**
- Touch **an event**, and then choose **the address.**

Change "leave now" alerts

If an event has a location, your Apple Watch will automatically send you a "leave now" notice based on the anticipated time it will take you to get there and the current traffic situation.

Do the following to select a certain time window, such as two hours before the event:

- Launch the **Calendar application on your iPhone.**
- Touch **the event.**
- Choose **Alert, then make a choice of another interval.**

Adjust calendar settings

You can choose which calendars will show up on your Apple Watch and alter the types of calendar notifications you obtain by doing the following:

- Launch **the Apple Watch application on your iPhone.**
- Touch **My Watch, then touch Calendar.**
- Choose **Custom beneath Notifications or Calendars.**

Capturing Ideas with Notes and Voice Dictation

With the use of the Voice Memos application on Apple Watch, you can have your personal notes recorded such that you will be able to listen to the notes anytime you like.

Record a voice memo

- Launch the **Voice Memos application on your Apple Watch.**
- Touch **the record icon.**
- Touch **the stop icon when you are ready to bring the recording to an end.**

Play a voice memo

- Launch **the Voice Memos application on your Apple Watch.**
- Touch **a recording on the voice Memos screen**, then touch **the play icon to play it.**
- You can choose to touch any of the skipping options (either forward or backward) respectively.
- To make a choice of an AirPlay device, **modify the name of the recording, or delete the recording, touch the More options, and then touch Edit Name or Delete.**

It is worth noting that the Voice memos you record on your Apple Watch instantly sync to your Mac, iPad, and any other iOS devices where you have signed in using the same Apple ID.

Time Management Tools: Stopwatch, Timer, and Alarms

Stopwatch

Events may be timed easily and accurately. The results can be shown as a list, a graph, or live on your watch face using Apple Watch's event timing capabilities. Full events can be timed using the device for up to 11 hours, and 55 minutes. The stopwatch is integrated into the Chronograph and Chronograph Pro watch faces.

Open and choose a stopwatch

- Launch **the Stopwatch application** on your Apple Watch, or **touch the stopwatch on your watch face** if you have added it or you have been using the Chronograph Pro watch face).
- To make a choice of another format, switch **to the Digital Crown. You can make a choice of Analog, Hybrid, or Digital.**

Start, stop, and reset the stopwatch

Launch the Stopwatch application on your Apple Watch, switch the Digital Crown to make a choice of a format, then do any of the following below;

- **Start:** Touch the **start icon.**
- **Record a lap**: Touch **the record icon.**
- **Record the final time**: Touch **its icon.**
- **Reset the stopwatch**: With the stopwatch halted, touch **the reset icon.**

The timing will then proceed even if you return to the watch face or launch other applications. Take a view of results on the display you made use of for timing, or alter displays so that you will be able to analyze your lap times and fastest/slowest laps (denoted with green and red) in the format you like to make use of.

Timers

Set timers on the Apple Watch

The Timers application on the Apple Watch can be of help in the tracking of time. You can configure various timers that aid in tracking time for up to 24 hours.

Quickly set a timer

- Launch the **Timer application on your Apple Watch.**
- If you would like to swiftly commence with the use of a timer, touch your preferred duration (such as 1, 3, or 5 minutes) or touch a timer you have just used beneath Recents.

When a timer trips off, you can touch the reset icon to commence a timer of the same duration.

Pause or end a timer

- With a timer running, launch the Timers application on your Apple Watch.
- Touch **the pause icon to pause**, touch **the play icon to resume**, or touch **the X icon to end the timer.**

Create a custom timer

- Launch the **Timer application on your Apple Watch.**
- Touch **the Create Timer icon.**
- Touch **hours, minutes, or seconds then switch the Digital Crown to modify where necessary.**
- Touch **Start.**

Create multiple timers

- Launch **the Timers application on your Apple Watch.**
- Create and launch **a timer.**
- Touch **the + icon** to go back to the Timers screen, then create and launch another timer.

To see your running timers on the Timers screen, tap the back symbol. To stop a timer, tap the pause icon. To restart it, tap the play icon. Swipe left, then press the **X button** to remove a running or stopped timer from the Timers interface.

Exploring the Find My App for People and Devices

Finding individuals who matter to you and letting them know where you are is easy with the Find Individuals app. You may easily find friends and family members on a map if they share their positions with you using an iPhone, iPad, or Apple Watch. Notifications can be set up to notify you when friends or relatives depart from or arrive at specific areas. It is worth noting that the Find People option may not be available for use in all regions.

Add a friend

- Launch **the Find People application on your Apple Watch.**

- Navigate down, then touch **Share My Location.**
- Touch **the Dictation, Contacts, or Keypad button to make a choice of a friend.**
- Choose **your preferred email address or phone number.**
- Make a choice of the duration you would like to share your location; an hour, until the end of the day, or indefinitely.

You can share your location with your friends, and they get a notification. They have the option of telling you where they are as well. When your buddy agrees to share their location, you may use the Find My app for iPhone, iPad, and Mac or the Find People app on Apple Watch to view their location in a list or on a map. If you would like to put an end to sharing your location with a friend, touch the **name of your friend on the Find People screen**, then touch **Stop Sharing**. If you would like to stop sharing your location with everyone, launch the Settings application on your Apple Watch, locate **Privacy & Security > Location Services**, and then switch off **Share My Location.** More on the use of Find My App has been covered in chapter 6 of this book discussing the built-in application.

Find Devices

The Find Devices application on the Apple Watch can help with locating Apple devices that may have been lost or misplaced.

Turn on Find My Network for your Apple Watch

When you enable Find My iPhone, your Apple Watch will already be configured if it is associated with your iPhone.

Make sure the Find My network is activated in order to locate your watch even when it is disconnected or powered off.

- Launch **the Settings application on your Apple Watch.**
- Touch y**our name**, then **navigate down until you are able to see your Apple Watch.**
- Touch **your watch name,** and then t**ouch Find My Watch.**
- Switch on **"Find My Network" if this has not been turned on just yet.**

See the location of a device

If your device is online, you will be able to have a view of its location in the Find Devices application. For devices that are supported, Find Devices can find the device even if the device is switched off, in Low Power Mode, or if Airplane Mode is switched on. **Launch the Find Device application on your Apple Watch, and then touch a device**

- **If the device can be found**: it will be displayed on the map so you will be able to see where it is. The approximate distance of the device, the time it last established a connection to either cellular or Wi-Fi, and the level of charge will be displayed at the top of the map. An approximate location will then be shown below the map.
- **If the device cannot be found:** You will see the "No location" beneath the name of the device. Beneath Notifications, switch on Notify When Found. You will get a notification once it has been found. If you would like to see devices that belong to members of your family group, navigate down to the lower part of the device and touch Show Family Devices.

Get directions to a device

You can get directions to the current location of a device in the Maps application on your Apple Watch.

- Launch **the Find Device application on your Apple Watch,** and then touch a **device you would like to have directions to.**
- Touch **Directions to open Maps.**
- Touch **the route to get directions from your location to the current location of the device.**

Receive a notification when you have left a device behind

You can get a notification when you've left your device behind to prevent you from losing it. Additionally, you may create Trusted Locations—areas where you can leave your smartphone alone without receiving a message.

- Launch **the Find Devices application on your Apple Watch**.
- Touch **the Device you would like to configure a notification for.**

- Beneath **Notifications**, choose **Notify When Left Behind**. Switch on **Notify When Left Behind, and then follow the instructions on the screen.**

If you would like to include a Trusted Location, you can make a choice of a suggested location, or touch **New Location,** choose **your preferred location on the map**, and then choose **Done**.

Mark a device as lost

You can lock your Mac or activate Lost Mode on your iPhone, iPad, or Apple Watch if your device is lost or stolen.

- Launch t**he Find Devices application on your Apple Watch, and then touch a device.**
- Touch **Lost Mode, and then switch on Lost Mode.**

When you mark a device as lost, the following will then happen;

- A confirmation email will be forwarded to your Apple ID email addresses.
- A message that shows that the device has been lost and how you should be contacted will be displayed on the Lock Screen of the device.
- Your device doesn't show alerts or make noise when you get messages or notifications, or if any alarms go off. Your device can still get phone calls and FaceTime calls.
- Apple Pay is disabled for your device. Any credit or debit card that you have linked to Apple Pay, student ID cards, and Express Transit cards will be taken off our device immediately. Credit, debit, and student ID cards will be removed immediately even if your device is offline. Express Transit cards will also be removed the next time your device gets an internet connection.
- For an iPhone, iPad, or Apple Watch, you view the current location of your device on the map and also be able to alter changes in its location.

Activity

1. Explore the use of calendars on your watch.
2. Capture your ideas and notes with the use of a voice memo on your watch.
3. Experiment with the use of a stopwatch, timer, and alarms.
4. Explore the Find My App for People and Devices you might have lost.

CHAPTER 9
ADVANCED CUSTOMIZATION AND SETTINGS

The Apple Watch Series 9 provides certain advanced customization options and configurations to tailor the device to your preferences and needs. In this chapter, you will learn about the various customizations and settings that you can make to your watch to ensure you get the best out of it.

Mastering Accessibility and Inclusivity Features

There are certain accessibility features in the Apple Watch Series 9 that help to ensure that you get better with the use of your watch. This feature helps to ensure that you are able to get the best out of your watch, ensuring you make use of all the features embedded in it for ease. In this section, you will learn about the very important features that you ought to know how to use as it pertains to your watch.

VoiceOver

VoiceOver helps you to make sure of your Apple Watch even if you cannot have a view of the display. Make use of simple gestures to get around the screen and also listen as VoiceOver speaks about each item you choose. **To have VoiceOver switched on simply;**

- Launch **the Settings application on your Apple Watch.**
- Locate **Accessibility > VoiceOver, and then switch on VoiceOver.**

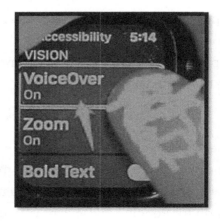

- To turn VoiceOver off, touch **the VoiceOver button twice.**

You can also choose to make use of your iPhone to switch on VoiceOver for your Apple Watch; open the Apple Watch application on your iPhone, touch My Watch, locate Accessibility, and then touch the VoiceOver option.

VoiceOver for Setup

VoiceOver can aid in the setting up of your Apple Watch; switch the Digital Crown thrice while setting up. Also, you may pair your Apple Watch with your iPhone and configure it using VoiceOver. Touch and hold the screen, then slide your finger around or swipe left or right to activate VoiceOver. To make the highlighted item active, double-tap it.

Below are step-by-step instructions for setting up the Apple Watch,

- If your Apple Watch is not switched on, switch it on by **holding down the side button which can be found beneath the Digital Crown.**
- On your Apple Watch, switch o**n VoiceOver by triple-clicking the Digital Crown.**
- Ensure your iPhone is close to your Apple Watch.
- On your iPhone, choose **Continue, and then make a couple-tap.**
- To attempt automatic pairing, point **the iPhone camera at the watch from around 6 inches away.** When you hear the pairing confirmation, proceed with the spoken prompts. If you have issues, you can attempt manual pairing from steps 7 to 13.
- On your iPhone, choose **Pair Apple Watch Manually, then make a double-tap.**
- On your Apple Watch, choose the **Info button in the lower right corner, then make a double-tap.**
- On your Apple Watch, choose your Apple Watch ID close to the upper part of the screen. You get to hear the unique identifier for your Apple Watch; it should be something like "Apple 52345".
- On your iPhone, make a choice of this same identifier, then make a double-tap.
- Choose **the six-digit pairing code on your Apple Watch to hear it.**
- Insert **the pairing code from your Apple Watch** on your iPhone with the use of the keyboard. You will feel the Apple Watch tap you when the connection is successful, and you will also hear "Your Apple Watch is paired." When pairing is

unsuccessful, tap to react to the alerts. You can try again after resetting both your Apple Watch and the Apple Watch app on your iPhone.

- On your iPhone, choose to **Restore from Backup** or **Set Up as New Apple Watch, then make a double-tap.**
- Proceed with the spoken prompts to go ahead with the configuration of your Apple Watch. After setup is complete, Apple Watch synchronizes with your iPhone. This takes some time; on your iPhone, hit Sync Progress to hear the status. Your Apple Watch is ready to use when you hear "sync complete" and the watch face appears. To view the features of the watch face, swipe left or right.

Control the Apple Watch with your iPhone

People who have physical and motor disabilities may find it much easier to gain control of their Apple Watch from the larger screen on the iPhone they have paired with their watch. With the use of Apple Watch mirroring, you can gain control of the Apple Watch by making use of assistive features like Voice Control and Switch Control and also make use of inputs which include voice commands, sound actions, head tracking, or external Made for iPhone switches as alternatives to touching the Apple Watch display.

To make use of this feature, follow the settings below;

- Launch the **Settings application on the paired iPhone.**
- Locate **Accessibility > Apple Watch Mirroring,** and then switch **on Apple Watch Mirroring.**

An image that helps to mirror your Apple Watch will then be displayed on your iPhone. Make use of the gestures on the mirrored image.

- **Scroll:** Move **the display either up or down**.
- **Swipe between screens**: Touch **the Digital Crown on the display.**
- **Press the side button**: Touch **the side button on the display.**
- **Make use of Siri:** Touch and **get hold of the Digital Crown on the display.**

Assistive Touch

With the use of Assistive Touch, you can make use of your Apple Watch if you are experiencing difficulties using the screen or pressing the buttons. The built-in sensors that are on the Apple Watch can aid in answering calls, controlling the on-screen pointer, and also the launching of a menu of actions- all with the use of hand gestures.

With the use of gestures with AssistiveTouch, you will be able to do the below actions;

- Tap the display
- Touch the switch on the Digital Crown
- Move between screens
- Hold the side button
- Access Notification Center, Control Center, and the App Switcher
- Display applications
- Use Apple Pay
- Make a confirmation of double clicks of the side button
- Activate Siri
- Run a Siri shortcut

Setting up Assistive Touch

- Open the **Settings application on your Apple Watch.**
- Locate **Accessibility > Assistive Touch, and then switch on Assistive Touch.**
- Touch **Hand gestures, and then switch on Hand gestures.**

Tap "Learn more" underneath the Hand Gestures switch, then tap each motion to see a description of how to use it. An interactive animation demonstrates how to execute and refine a gesture when you tap it. You can also choose to open the Apple Watch application on your iPhone, touch My Watch, locate Accessibility > Assistive Touch, and then switch on Assistive Touch.

Using Assistive Touch with Apple Watch

With the use of Assistive Touch and Hand gestures switched on, move through your Apple Watch with the use of the following default gestures;

- **Pinch:** Forward
- **Double-Pinch:** Back
- **Clench:** Tap
- **Double-Clench:** Show the Action Menu

For instance, when you have the meridian face being displayed, make use of Assistive Touch with the Activity application and follow the steps below;

- Double-Clench to activate **Assistive Touch**. A highlight will then be displayed around the Music complication.
- Pinch **three times to get to the Activity complication, then clench to touch it.**
- When the Activity application opens, double-clench **to display the Action Menu.**
- Pinch once to **choose the System action,** pinch once more to choose the **Scroll Up action, and then clench to select it.**
- Clench to move to the following screen.
- Double-pinch to display **the Action Menu.** Pinch to move to the front through the actions; double-pinch to go back.
- Choose the **Press Crown action**, then clench once to go back to the watch face.

Use the Motion Pointer

With the Motion Pointer, you may tilt your Apple Watch up and down and side to side to operate it in addition to pinching and clenching.

Use the Motion Pointer, for instance, to explore the Stopwatch app by doing the following:

- With the watch face showing, double-clench in order to get the **Assistive Touch activated.**

- Double-clench once more to display the Action Menu. The Press Crown action will then be chosen.
- Clench to make a choice of the **Press Crown action** and also to launch the Home screen.
- Double-clench to **display the Action Menu**, pinch to go to the interaction action, then clench to touch it. Motion Pointer ought to be chosen now.
- Clench to switch on **the Motion Pointer.** A cursor will then be displayed on the screen.
- Shake the watch to position the cursor at the lower edge of the screen to move down.
- Hold the cursor over the stopwatch application for a little while to have it open.
- Hold the cursor over **the start button to touch it.**
- If you would like to go back to the watch face, double-clench to display the Action Menu, pinch to choose the **Press Crown action, and then clench to touch it.**

Use quick actions

You can respond more quickly when your Apple Watch displays an alert. For instance, a popup informs you that you can double-pinch to answer an incoming call. Additionally, you may start a workout when Apple Watch detects exercise-like behavior, snooze an alarm or stop a timer using quick actions, and capture a picture when the Camera app's viewfinder and shutter button are visible. The steps below can be used to enable or disable rapid actions.

- Launch **the Settings application on your Apple Watch.**
- Locate **Accessibility > Quick Actions, then choose your preferred option.**

You can make a choice of having quick actions available all the time, available only when AssistiveTouch has been enabled, or off. You can make a choice of also choosing Full appearance (a banner shows and the action button will then be highlighted) or Minimal appearance (the action button is highlighted with no banner).

Adjust AssistiveTouch settings

The actions associated with the pinch, clench, and Motion Pointer gestures can be modified, and the Motion Pointer's sensitivity can be changed.

Choose one of the following actions from the Accessibility > AssistiveTouch menu in the Settings app on your Apple Watch:

- **Customize gestures:** Touch **Hand Gestures, touch a gesture, then make a choice of an action or a Siri shortcut.**
- **Customize the Motion Pointer**: Touch the **Motion Pointer, then alter settings for sensitivity, activation time, movement tolerance, and hot edges.**
- **Scanning style**: Make a choice between automatic scanning, where actions are instantly highlighted one after the other, or Manual, where you can make use of gestures to move between actions.
- **Appearance**: Switch on **High Contrast** in order to make the Highlight much bolder. Touch **Color t**o make a choice between another highlight colors.
- **Customize Menu:** Add favorite actions, modify the position and size of the Action Menu, and alter the auto-scroll speed.
- **Confirm with AssistiveTouch:** Switch on to make use of the AssistiveTouch for the confirmation of payments with the passcode or any time double-clicking the side button is needed.

You can also choose to launch the Apple Watch on your iPhone, touch **My Watch, and then locate Accessibility> AssistiveTouch.**

Use a braille display with Voiceover

Numerous worldwide braille tables and refreshable braille displays are supported by the Apple Watch. To read VoiceOver output, including braille that has been contracted and has not, you can attach a Bluetooth wireless braille display. The braille display shows the text in context when you modify it, and your changes are automatically transformed from braille to printed text. When VoiceOver is used, you may additionally employ a braille display with input keys to operate your Apple Watch.

Connect a braille display

- Switch **on the braille display.**
- Locate **Settings > Accessibility > VoiceOver > Braille, and then make a choice of the display.**

Change the braille display settings

- On **the Apple Watch, locate Settings > Accessibility > VoiceOver > Braille.**
- **Configure any of the following;**

Setting	Description
Output	Configure the braille display output to an uncontracted six-dot, uncontracted eight-dot, or contracted braille.
Input	Make a choice of the input method for inserting braille on the display-uncontracted six-dot, uncontracted eight-dot, or contracted braille. You can also choose to switch to Automatic Translation.
Word Wrap	Wrap words to the next line.
Alert Display Duration	Modify the duration that an alert is visible on your braille display.
Braille Tables	Include tables to the Braille Table rotor.

Using a Bluetooth keyboard with VoiceOver

You can have a Bluetooth keyboard connected to control VoiceOver output. Hold down the modifier key of the keyboard and type to go through Apple Watch with the use of VoiceOver.

Connect a Bluetooth keyboard

- Launch **the Settings application on your Apple Watch.**
- Locate **Accessibility > VoiceOver > Keyboards.**
- Place the keyboard in pairing mode, navigate to the lower part of the screen, and then touch the keyboard beneath Devices.

Change the keyboard Settings;

- Launch **the Settings application on your Apple Watch.**
- Locate **Accessibility > VoiceOver > Keyboards.**
- **Choose any of the following;**

Setting	Description
Phonetic feedback	Choose to listen to characters and phonics or phonetics alone.
Typing feedback	Make a choice of hearing characters, words, or characters and words as you type on the Bluetooth keyboard.
Modifier keys	Select the modifier keys on a physical keyboard that must be pressed in order to enable VoiceOver key commands. Control + Option and Caps Lock are available options that can be used.

Navigate with the use of the keyboard

Make use of the following keys for ease of navigation with the use of the Bluetooth keyboard;

Setting	Action
Right Arrow key	Move to the next item
Left Arrow key	Go to the previous item
Modifier key + Down Arrow key	Read out the character or phonetics of the chosen item from left to right
Modifier key + Up Arrow key	Read out the character or phonetics of the chosen item from right to left.
Modifier key + Space bar	Touch chosen item

Use Zoom

Make use of Zoom to enlarge whatever you have on the Apple Watch display.

Switch on Zoom

- Launch the **Settings application on your Apple Watch.**
- Locate **Accessibility > Zoom, and then switch on Zoom.**

You can also make use of your iPhone to switch on Zoom for your Apple Watch -launch the Apple Watch application on your iPhone, touch My Watch, touch Accessibility, then touch Zoom, or you can also choose to make use of the Accessibility shortcut.

Controlling Zoom

Once you have switched on Zoom, you can do all of these actions on your Apple Watch.

- **Zoom in or out:** Tap the **Apple Watch display twice with two fingers.**
- **Move around (pan):** Move the **display with two fingers.** You can also choose to **switch the Digital Crown to pan over the whole page, left-right, and up-down.** The little Zoom button that displays shows you where you are on the page.
- **Use the Digital Crown normally instead of panning:** Touch t**he display once with two fingers** to move between making use of the Digital Crown to pan and making use of the Digital Crown the way it works without Zoom being on for instance, moving through a list or zooming a map.
- **Adjust magnification:** Touch **twice and hold with two fingers,** then move your fingers **up or down on the display**. To reduce magnification, touch **the plus or minus button on the Maximum Zoom Level slider.**

Tell time with haptic feedback

When it is in silent mode, the Apple Watch can tap out the time on your wrist with various distinct taps. Get any of the following done;

- Launch **the Settings application on your Apple Watch.**
- Touch **Clock, move down, and then touch Taptic time.**
- Switch on **Taptic Time, then make a choice of a setting; Digits, Terse, or Morse code**. Hours and minutes are shown in the following ways;
  - **Digits:** Apple Watch long taps for every 10 hours, short taps for each following hour, long taps for every 10 minutes, then short taps for each following minute.
  - **Terse**: Apple Watch long taps for every five hours, short taps for the rest of the hours, then long taps for each quarter hour.
  - **Morse code:** Apple Watch touches each digit of the time in Morse code.

- If you would like to have a feel of a haptic version of the time, touch and hold two fingers on the watch face. Taptic Time can also work when the Always On Display is dimmed.

If VoiceOver is turned on, switch on Taptic Time by tapping twice on the watch face while the display is inactive. You can also choose to configure Taptic Time on the iPhone. Launch the Apple Watch application on your iPhone, touch **My Watch**, navigate to **Clock > Taptic Time,** and then switch it on.

Note: If the Apple Watch has been configured to always speak the time, Taptic Time will not function. Go to **Settings > Clock** to enable Control with Silent Mode, then select **Speak Time to enable Taptic Time.**

Use of RTT

A technique called real-time text (RTT) allows you to send audio along with your text. When you're not near your iPhone, Apple Watch with cellular can communicate through RTT if you have trouble speaking or hearing. There are no other devices needed because Apple Watch employs built-in Software RTT that you set up in the Apple Watch app. Not all carriers or regions offer RTT capability. In the US, Apple Watch delivers distinctive characters or tones to the operator during emergency calls. Depending on where you are, the operator's capacity to hear or respond to these tones may change. Apple makes no promises regarding the operator's capacity to accept or reply to an RTT call.

Switch on RTT

- Launch the **Apple Watch application on your iPhone**.
- Touch **My Watch, locate Accessibility > RTT, and then switch on RTT.**
- Touch the **Relay Number,** and then insert the phone number to utilize for relay calls with the use of RTT.
- Switch on Send Immediately to send each character as you are typing. Switch off in order to complete messages prior to your sending.

Start an RTT call

- Open the **Apple Watch application on your iPhone.**
- Touch **My Watch, locate Accessibility > RTT, and then switch on RTT.**

- Touch **the Relay Number, and then insert the phone number to use for relay calls with the use of RTT.**
- Switch on **Send Immediately** in order to send each character as you type. Switch off to complete messages prior to sending.

Start an RTT call

- Launch **the Phone application on your Apple Watch.**
- Touch **Contacts,** and then switch **the Digital Crown to scroll.**
- Touch **the Contacts** you would like to call, navigate down, and then touch the **RTT button.**
- Scribble a message, touch a reply from the list, or you can also choose to send an emoji.

It is worth noting that you will be notified if the other person on the phone call has not enabled RTT.

Answer an RTT call

- When you can hear or feel the call notification, lift your wrist to see the person calling.
- Touch the Answer button, navigate down, and then touch the **RTT button.**
- Scribble a message, touch a **reply from the list,** or you can also choose to **send an emoji.**

Do note, however, that Scribble is unavailable in all languages.

Edit default replies

With just a tap, you may respond to an RTT call on an Apple Watch when you place or receive one.

Use these steps to make more of your own responses:

- Launch **the Apple Watch application on your iPhone.**
- Touch **My Watch, locate Accessibility > RTT, and then touch Default Replies.**
- Touch **Add reply, insert your reply, and then touch done.**

Choose Edit in the Default Replies box to edit, delete, or rearrange the order of existing replies.

Accessibility audio settings on Apple Watch

If you would like to hear both the left and the right audio signals out of the two audio channels on speakers or headphones connected to your Apple Watch, switch on **Mono Audio**. You can also alter the left-right balance of your Apple Watch audio if stereo or mono. You can also alter AirPods configurations such that it is more accessible.

Change mono audio and balance settings

Launch the Settings application on your Apple Watch, then, beneath Hearing, get any of the following done;

- **Switch from stereo to mono audio:** Switch on **Mono Audio.**
- **Adjust the audio balance**: Touch the **L or R button beneath Mono Audio.**

You can also open the Apple Watch application on your iPhone, touch My Watch, touch Accessibility, and then switch on Mono Audio and modify the audio balance.

Change AirPods settings

You can alter press speed and press-and-hold duration settings for the AirPods you see with the use of your Apple Watch. You can also switch on noise cancellation on AirPods Pro when you have one of your AirPods in just one ear.

- Launch the **Settings application on your Apple Watch.**
- Navigate to **Accessibility > AirPods, choose your AirPods, then pick settings.**

You can also launch the Apple Watch application on your iPhone, touch My Watch, and then locate **Accessibility > AirPods.**

Show HomePod transcriptions

Apple Watch is also able to display transcriptions for any HomePod announcements when the two devices make use of the same Apple ID.

- Launch the **Settings application on your Apple Watch.**
- Locate **Accessibility, then switch on Show Audio Transcriptions.**

Turn on headphone notifications

If you would like to protect your hearing, your Apple Watch is able to send a notification if you happen to have been listening to loud headphone audio for a long time to affect your hearing.

- Launch t**he Settings application on your Apple Watch.**
- Locate **Accessibility, then switch on Headphone Notifications.**

Type to speak on Apple Watch

With the use of Live Speech, you can type and have your words spoken aloud, both in person and on the phone, and even on FaceTime audio calls.

Set up Live Speech

- Launch the **Settings application on your Apple Watch.**
- Navigate to **Accessibility > Live Speech, then touch Voices.**
- Make a choice of your preferred voice, then touch **Speak Sample** to listen to it. If you would like to make use of the voice, touch **Download, then touch Use Voice.**
- If you would like to configure the Accessibility Shortcut to switch on Live Speech, navigate to **Settings > Accessibility > Accessibility Shortcut, and then select Live Speech.**

Type to speak

- Triple-click the **Digital Crown**, and then what you would like to have spoken or make a choice of your preferred phrase.
- Touch **Speak to have your phrase spoken.**

People will then listen to your words spoken in the conversation if you are either on a phone or on a FaceTime audio call. If this doesn't happen, they will proceed from the speaker on your Apple Watch.

Display and Sound Customization

The display and customization of sound is a very important aspect of the use of the Apple Watch. In this section, you will learn how to personalize the sound and display of your Apple Watch.

Open the Settings application on your Apple Watch, then touch Display & Brightness to alter the following;

- **Brightness**: Touch **the Brightness controls** to alter, or touch the slider, and then switch **the Digital Crown.**

- **Text Size**: the size of the text helps you to see all in your Apple Watch easily when you personalize it. Touch **Text Size**, then touch **the letters or switch the Digital Crown.**

- **Bold Text:** Switch **on Bold Text.**

You can also choose to make these alterations on your iPhone. Lunah the Apple Watch application on your iPhone, touch **My Watch, touch Display & Brightness, and then alter brightness and text.**

Adjust sound

- Launch the **Settings application on your Apple Watch.**
- Touch **Sounds & Haptics.**
- Touch t**he volume controls beneath Alert Volume or touch the slider, then switch the Digital Crown to modify it.**

As an alternative, you can with your iPhone, launch the Apple Watch application, touch **Sounds & Haptics, and then move the Alert Volume slider.** You can also choose to reduce loud sounds coming from headphones connected to your Apple Watch. In the Settings application, navigate to **Sounds & Haptics > Headphones Safety, then switch on Reduce Loud Sounds.**

Adjust haptic intensity

You can alter the strength of the haptics or wrist taps that Apple Watches makes use of for notifications and alerts.

- Launch the **Settings application on your Apple Watch.**
- Touch **Sounds & Haptics, then switch on Haptic Alerts.**

- Make your preferred choice between Default Or Prominent.

Privacy and Security Essentials

Privacy and security are important aspects of making use of any smart device which also includes your Apple Watch. In this section, you will learn about the various ways in which you can be security conscious and also be able to further protect your watch.

Recover Apple Watch

If your Apple Watch shows an animation displaying a watch and iPhone being brought close to each other, follow the steps below;

- Position your iPhone close to your Apple Watch. Your iPhone ought to have iOS 15.4 or later, be connected to Wi-Fi with Bluetooth switched on, and be unlocked.
- Put your Apple Watch on its charger.
- Click **the side button two times** then follow the steps that are displayed on the iPhone.

If you forget your Apple Watch passcode

If your Apple Watch is disabled due to the fact that you forgot your passcode or inserted an incorrect passcode too many times, you are able to rest it on your Apple Watch. If Erase Data is switched on, the data on your Apple Watch will be erased after 10 failed passcode attempts.

Reset your Apple Watch

- Place your **Apple Watch** on its charger, then touch and hold the side button until the slider is being displayed.
- Tap and hold **the Digital Crown** to display the Erase all content and settings screen.
- Touch **Reset, and then touch Reset once more to confirm.**
- When the process has been completed, configure your watch all over again.

Update Apple Watch software

You can choose to update your Apple Watch software by searching for updates in the Apple Watch application on your iPhone.

- Launch **the Apple Watch application on your iPhone.**
- Touch **My Watch, navigate to General > Software Update**, and then, if you notice that an update is available, touch **Download and install it.**

You can also launch the Settings application on your Apple Watch, then navigate to General > Software Update.

Protecting a lost Apple Watch

If you happen to lose your Apple Watch, you can protect it by putting it in lost mode.

Find your Apple Watch

- Launch **the Apple Watch application on your iPhone.**
- Touch **My Watch, then touch All Watches.**
- Touch the caution **sign close to your watch, then touch Find My Apple Watch.**
- In the Find My application on your iPhone, touch your watch to have a view of its location on a map. If the map says your Apple Watch is at your location, touch Play Sound.

Mark your Apple Watch as lost

When you mark your Apple Watch as being lost, your watch will be locked with a passcode so that other people will not be able to gain access to your personal information, and the ability to pay with Apple Pay making use of credit or debit cards in Wallet will be suspended.

- Launch the **Apple Watch application on your iPhone.**
- Touch **My Watch, then touch All Watches.**
- Touch the caution icon close to your watch, then touch **Find My Watch.**
- In the Find My application on your iPhone, touch **Activate beneath Mark As Lost, then touch Continue.**

- Insert a phone number if you would like the person who is able to locate your Apple Watch to contact you.
- Touch **Next, t**hen insert a message that will be displayed on your **Apple Watch when anyone is able to locate it.**
- Touch **Next**, then touch **Activate t**o get your Apple Watch marked as lost.

If you would like to erase a lost Apple Watch, from step 3 above, do the following;

- In the Find My application on your iPhone, touch **your watch,** then touch **Erase This Device.**

Tailoring Notifications and Control Center

Applications are able to send notifications to ensure that you are informed about meeting invitations, messages, noise alerts, etc. Your Apple Watch can show notifications as you get them, but it is not compulsory for you to reply immediately as it is saved so that you can view it later.

Respond to a notification when it arrives

- If you hear or feel a notification, lift your wrist to check it. The way the notification looks is based on if the display is active or idle.
  - ○ **Active display:** a little banner will be displayed at the top of the display.
  - ○ **Idle display:** a full-screen notification will be displayed.
- Touch the notification to read it.
- If you would like to erase a notification, move down on it. You can also choose to scroll to the bottom of the notification, and then touch Dismiss.

Change notification settings on the Apple Watch

By default, the notification settings for the applications on an Apple Watch that you configure for yourself show the settings on your iPhone. All the same, you can choose to customize how certain applications will show notifications.

Choose how applications send notifications

- Launch the **Apple Watch application on your iPhone.**

- Touch **My Watch, then choose Notifications.**
- Touch the application, for instance, Messages, touch Custom, then make a preferred choice. The available options may include;
    - **Allow Notifications:** The application shows notifications in the Notification Center.
    - **Send to Notification Center**: Notifications are usually sent directly to the Notification Center without your Apple Watch making any form of sound or showing the notification.
    - **Notifications off**: The application sends no notifications.
- **Notification grouping: Choose how notifications for the application are grouped. The options include;**
    - **Off**: Notifications are not grouped.
    - **Automatically:** Your Apple Watch makes use of information from the application to make another group.
    - **By App**: All the application notifications are grouped.

Change notification settings directly on your Apple Watch

You can control other notification preferences straight from your Apple Watch by moving left on a notification and touching the more options. The options available include;

- **Mute 1 hour or Mute Today**: For the next hour or for the remaining hours of the day, notifications are sent straight to the Notification Center without your Apple Watch creating a sound or displaying the notification. If you would like to see and hear these notification alerts again, move **left on a notification**, touch *** then choose **UnMute**.
- **Turn off:** in this option, the application will not send any notification. If you would like to enable notifications from the application, launch the Apple Watch application on your iPhone, touch M**y Watch, touch Notifications, touch the application** you would like to alter, and then touch **Allow Notifications.**

Show notifications on the lock screen

You can choose just how notifications show on your lock screen.

- Launch the **Settings application on your Apple Watch.**
- Touch **Notifications**
- Make your preferred choice from the following options;

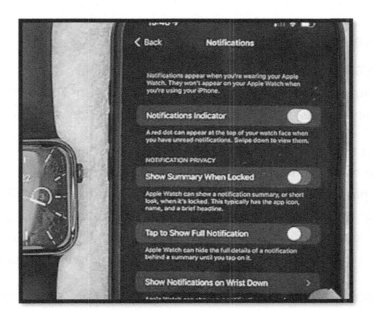

- ○ **Show Summary When locked:** with the use of this option, your Apple Watch displays a notification summary- or short look anytime it is locked. The summary includes the name and the icon of the application sending the notification and also a brief headline of what the notification is about.
- ○ **Tap to Show Full Notification**: When you lift your wrist to view a notification, you will be shown a quick summary, then complete details a few seconds later. For instance, when you get a message, you will get to see who the message is from first, then the message will be displayed. Switch on this option if you would like to stop the full notification from being displayed unless you touch it.
- ○ **Show Notifications on Wrist Down:** By default, notifications are not shown on your Apple Watch when your wrist is lying down. Switch on these options to

ensure notifications are displayed even when your Apple Watch is shifted away from you.

Control Center

The control center provides you with an easy opportunity to check your battery, silence your watch, make your preferred choice of focus, turn your Apple Watch into a flashlight, place your Apple Watch in Airplane Mode, switch on theater mode, and lots more.

Open or close the Control Center

- **Open the Control Center**: Tap the **side button just once.**
- **Close Control:** With the use of the Control Center, turn your wrist away from you or as an alternative, you can also choose to tap the side button once more.

There are various things that can be done in the Control Center which include; turning cellular either on or off, connecting or disconnecting from Wi-Fi, switching School Time either on or off, pinning your iPhone, checking your battery percentage, silencing Apple Watch, locking your watch with the use of a passcode, choosing a focus or Do Not Disturb, turning off sleep focus, turning the flashlight either on or off, turning on the water lock, making a preferred choice of audio output, checking headphone volume, etc.

Check Control Center Status

Small icons at the upper part of the Control Center show the status of some settings; for instance, the fact that your Apple Watch is connected to cellular, your location is being used by an application, and certain features like Airplane Mode and Do Not Disturb are switched on. If you would like to see the status icon, touch the side button to launch the Control Center. If you would like to get details, touch the icons.

Rearrange Control Center

You can choose to rearrange the buttons in the Control Center by going through the steps below;

- Tap the **side button i**n order to open the **Control Center.**
- Move to the lower corner of the Control Center, then touch **Edit.**

- Touch and **hold a button,** then move it to another location.
- Touch **Done** when you are through.

Remove Control Center buttons

You can choose to remove the buttons in the Control Center by following the following steps;

- Touch the **side button to launch the Control Center.**
- Navigate to the lower part of the Control Center, then touch **Edit.**
- Tap **the red icon** in the corner of the button you would like to remove.
- When you are through touch **Done.**

To restore a button you have once removed, launch the **Control Center**, touch **Edit**, and then touch the **Green icon** in the corner of the button you would like to bring back. Touch **Done** when you are through. In the sections below you will learn about some of the things that you can do in the Control Center;

Flashlight

You can make use of the flashlight to give light to a darkened door lock, give an alert to other people when you are not around in the evening, and give light to objects that are close to you which will ensure the preservation of your night vision.

- **Switch on the flashlight:** Touch **the side button to open Control Center**, then touch the **flash icon**. Move to the left side to choose your preferred mode.
- **Adjust the brightness**: Switch the **Digital Crown either up or down.**
- **Turn off the flashlight**: Tap the **Digital Crown or the side button**, or you can also choose to move down from the upper part of the watch face.

Disconnect from Wi-Fi

You can choose to disconnect from a Wi-Fi network temporarily and also on Apple Watch models with cellular, making use of an available cellular connection instead directly from the Control Center. Your Apple Watch will disconnect temporarily from the Wi-Fi network. If you have an Apple Watch cellular, the cellular connection will immediately become active when there is coverage. When you choose to leave and later go back to the place where you were initially connected to Wi-Fi, your Apple Watch instantly joins that network once more unless you have forgotten it on your iPhone.

Turn on Silent Mode

You can choose to silence your Apple Watch at any point in time. All you have to do is touch the side button to launch the **Control Center and then touch the bell icon.** It is worth noting that if your Apple Watch is charging, alarms and timers will still give a sound even when it is in silent mode. Whenever you get a notification, you can quickly mute your Apple Watch by simply laying the palm of your hand on the watch display for about three seconds. You will feel a tap to confirm that the mute has been switched on. Ensure you switch on Cover to Mute on your Apple Watch; open the Settings application, touch **Sounds, and then switch on Cover to Mute**.

Ping and find your iPhone

On the Apple Watch Series 9, you can make use of Precision Finding to ping your nearby iPhone and get directions to it.

- On your Apple Watch Series 9, touch **the side button to open the Control Center,** then touch the phone icon. Your iPhone will then play a sound and, if your Apple Watch Series 9 is actually within range, the screen will show a general heading and distance to your iPhone-77 feet, for instance.
- If you would like to play a sound on your iPhone as you are tracking it down, touch **the phone icon in the lower right corner.**
- Take after the heading being displayed on the screen, and make all the adjustments as needed as the heading moves. When you are quite close to your iPhone, the screen of the watch will change to green and the iPhone will then ping twice. If your phone is not within range, attempt to make use of Find My from icloud.com. It is worth noting Precision is not available in all regions hence not everyone will be able to use it.

Ping your Apple Watch

You can make use of your iPhone with iOS 17 to help with the location of your Apple Watch if it is close by.

- Launch the **settings application on your iPhone.**
- Touch **Control Center,** move down, then touch the **green icon close to Ping My Watch.**
- When you want to ping your Apple Watch, move down from the upper-right corner of your iPhone to launch the **Control Center**, then touch the **phone icon.**

It is worth noting that if you have more than just one Apple Watch, the sound will play on the watch that is chosen in All Watches in the Apple Watch application on your iPhone. You can also make use of Find My to play a sound on your Apple Watch.

Activity

1. Configure the display and sound in your watch.
2. Check out the control center and personalize it.
3. Check out the various accessibility features in your watch.

CHAPTER 10
TROUBLESHOOTING AND MAINTENANCE
Navigating Common Hiccups and Glitches

Apple Watches are often known for their amazing features and fantastic performance. Nevertheless, with all of the high-quality designs they possess, certain spontaneous issues can arise that can lead to the user of the watch being highly frustrated. These issues can be caused by various factors but most of them are usually linked to software glitches, internal settings, and also hardware malfunctioning. Immediately you notice that the ACTH isn't responding as it ought to, a feeling of dread can surface as you search for answers online or search through the fine print in your user manual. Certain remedies are easy to find with immediate effect while others are not so easy to find hence there will be a need to continue to persist and overwhelm your best efforts. In the list below, you will learn about some of the most frustrating Apple Watch issues and also how to get them fixed.

Apple Watch won't charge

Although an Apple Watch can last for up to 18 hours, these numbers mean just a little once you are unable to charge your device. In most cases, users often put the blame on faulty cables and weak connections, but also there are times when the solution can be just right in front of you or even buried within.

Below are possible ways to fix the problem of an Apple Watch not charging;

- **Know your symbols and icons:** this might sound and look very simple, but the first thing you will like to be sure of is if your Apple Watch is actually not charging in its real sense. This means that you have a knowledge of the difference between the red and the green lightning bolt symbols. Green means charge and red means that no source of power has been detected.
- **Force restart:** If your Apple Watch has just a little battery life left, you can attempt to force a restart that can reset the charging error. This can be done by pressing and holding the side button and digital crown together for about 10 seconds. Once

the Apple logo has been displayed, let go of the button and allow the restart to commence.

- **Clean both the Apple Watch and charger**: Since the Apple Watch charges with the use of a magnetic connection, there is every possibility that dirt may be interfering with your power connection. Clean the rear of your Apple Watch and the charging dock and check if you have been able to resolve the issue.
- **Try an official Apple Watch charger if you are not using one**: If you happen to be using a third-party Apple Watch charger, attempt to make use of the charger and cable that you bought with your device. There are times that third-party accessories can cause issues as regards compatibility.

Unable to connect to Wi-Fi

The Apple Watch Series 9 has the ability to maintain an independent Wi-Fi connection. This means that even if your iPhone is not within reach, your watch should still be able to access certain features like calls, emails, and messages with the use of the internet. Even though this is what is expected, there are times when your watch will just be unable to establish a connection with a wireless network.

Below are steps you can try to fix an Apple Watch that cannot connect to Wi-Fi;

- **Turn Wi-Fi off and on**: If this specific Wi-Fi connection has worked before, a simple Wi-Fi refresh may be all that is needed. Move up on your Apple Watch in order to open the Control Center, touch the Wi-Fi logo to switch it off, and then touch it once more to bring it back on. Pause for a few minutes and check for a possible Wi-Fi connection.
- **Forget Wi-Fi network**: One other way to solve this problem is for you to re-establish a Wi-Fi connection totally. Launch the Settings application on your Apple Watch, choose Wi-Fi, then make a choice of your preferred network from the list available, and then touch Forget. Switch your Wi-Fi off and on once more, and then attempt to establish a reconnection to a network of your choice.
- **Incompatible Wi-Fi networks**: If you have gone out of your usual Wi-Fi location, there will be a need for you to establish a connection with a new Wi-Fi network.

Apps continue to crash and freeze

One of the most annoying problems a user of an Apple Watch can experience is when the application they love to use the most keeps crashing and freezing. This can also include loading screens that never end, unresponsive commands, or applications that will not open or close at all. All of these obstacles can cause a disruption in system functionality, making it quite impossible to get any other thing done.

Below are steps to fixing the Apple Watch that will keep crashing and freezing;

- **Reopen the application**: If your Apple Watch still happens to be responsive but you cannot successfully open an app that crashes, you can attempt closing it and opening it once more. To get this done, touch the Side Button, navigate through the list of active applications, find the application that is affected, move the app from right to left, and then touch the big red icon. With this, the application should have closed, you can then try to open it again.
- **Force close the app:** If the application you are attempting to fix has frozen your Apple Watch totally this will mean you are most likely inside the very application hence there will be a need for you to force close the application. Touch the Digital Crown, choose the app you would like to force close, touch the hold the side button, and let go when the Power Down menu shows. Now tap and hold the Digital Crown once more until the app leaves.
- **Delete the app**: if the problem of the application still persists, it may be time for you to delete and reinstall the application. To get an app deleted, touch the Digital Crown until all of your applications show on the Home Screen. Touch and hold the display until the View Options screen shows, choose Edit Applications, and then touch the Delete button followed by the confirmation to delete the application. Once the deletion has been completed you can now reinstall the application from the App Store.

An unresponsive screen

The issue of a screen not responding can be one of the scariest problems you may face. As the basic interface of your device. You are going to have quite a hard time inputting commands or troubleshooting solutions if your screen no longer responds to various actions being done on it. This can lead to the total inability to make use of your Apple Watch thereby rendering the device totally useless until a fix has been found.

Below are steps to follow to solve the problem of an unresponsive Apple Watch screen;

- **Force restart**: A force restart is the very first thing that should be done to an unresponsive screen. Touch the hold down the Digital Crown and the side button for about 10 seconds. Pause a little for the Apple logo to be displayed then let go of the buttons. The device will restart and your screen will be active again.
- **Apps and updates:** if a pattern comes up and then your screen becomes unresponsive within a certain application alone, you can consider updating the app or uninstalling it totally. As an alternative, you can also check for a WatchOS update if the problem continues to be software-related.
- **Screen protectors**: Apple doesn't sell screen protectors for their watches hence if you are making use of a third-party protector, this can be the cause of your problem. Take off the protector and see if your screen responds.
- **Obstructions:** Just like the screen protector causing interference, if you are wearing gloves or your fingers are somewhat covered, this can also cause the screen to be unresponsive to your actions. Make use of a clean naked hand and check if the problem vanishes.

Notifications are not appearing

The notifications you get on your Apple Watch are one of the most useful features of the watch. Users are able to stay informed and connected to the world without having to move around with their phones in busy circumstances. Nevertheless, when your Apple Watch suddenly stops sending notifications, this can lead to you missing important updates, which could lead to time-sensitive consequences.

Follow the steps below to solve problems of notifications not appearing;

- **Lost connection**: The most common cause of notifications not appearing on your Apple Watch is a loss of connectivity between your iPhone and Apple Watch. If you happen to see a red iPhone icon, this means the connection has been lost. Get the devices close to each other and repair them through the Bluetooth setting in both your iPhone and Apple Watch.

- **Enable app notifications**: In case you have mistakenly switched off app notifications, you can reactivate the configuration by opening the Apple Watch app on your iPhone. Go to the Notifications tab, choose Allow Notifications, and toggle the specific application you would like to get notifications from.
- **Disable Wrist detection**: Wrist detection helps to lock your Apple Watch instantly when you are no longer wearing it leading to notifications being sent to your iPhone alone. If you would like to switch this feature off, navigate to your Settings application on your Apple Watch, choose Passcode, and disable Wrist Detection.
- **Force restart:** If all else fails, you can attempt restarting your Apple Watch by touching and holding the Side Button and Digital Crown until the Apple logo is seen.

Apple Watch is getting hot

Basically, the normal conditions for an Apple Watch are between 32 - 95 degrees Fahrenheit or 0 - 35 degrees Celsius. If the device becomes too warm, it may lead to the system slowing down, malfunctioning, or in very rare cases, suffering total damage. Away from the Apple Watch itself, a warm bodily accessory is also very uncomfortable to wear hence its best that you prevent your device from being overheated.

Below are steps that should be considered when you want to fix the issue of the Apple Watch becoming hot;

- **A cool storage location:** Almost everyone has that habit of leaving their accessories in the car, or in a place where it can come in contact with direct sunlight within the house. An Apple Watch ought to be kept in a shaded area, one that is not humid within temperatures of 4 to 113 degrees Fahrenheit. When next you pick up your Apple Watch and it feels so hot, you might have to reconsider your storage location.
- **Charging increases heat:** When your Apple Watch is charging and plugged into a source of power, it will create heat as the battery is being charged. Just like the issue with the storage location, you can also reduce these temperatures by making use of a power outlet in a cool area, but for the most part, you also should wait for your Apple Watch to reduce in temperature before you start using it.

- **Remove your Apple Watch**: If your Apple Watch gets really hot beyond use, and it is also followed by a red thermometer on the display showing above-normal temperatures, you can think of removing it from your wrist. The reason for the temperature increase can be a result of your current environment and also your body temperature.

Battery drains too fast

Just like your Apple Watch not charging well, a battery that drains way too fast can be very frustrating. However, once you are sure that the battery is not damaged physically, the solution might be as easy as some optimization configurations.

Below are ways by which you can fix the problem of battery draining too fast;

- **Wake Screen time**: With the Wake Screen configuration being activated, each time you lift your wrist, your Apple Watch will come on. The display can remain active for about 70 seconds, which can consume a lot of power. Bring a reduction to this time by launching the Settings application on your Apple Watch, choosing Display & Brightness, then Wake Duration, and then altering the value to 15 seconds.
- **Turn off push notifications**: if you happen to get lots of notifications during the day, it might be a great option to switch off app alerts. Launch the Apple Watch on your iPhone, choose Notifications, and then disable the applications you feel are not so important.
- **Turn off background refresh**: Your iPhone and Apple Watch will transmit information back and forth non-stop. With that being said, certain application synchronizations may not provide enough rewards to justify their battery consumption. Launch the Apple Watch application on your iPhone, find Background Application Refresh in your General Settings, and switch off apps that are not wanted.

Digital Crown is not working

The Digital Crown on your Apple Watch can be described as an alternative means by which you can interact with your device. Users are able to move through the various menus, modify system volume, and even send out emergency SOS alerts. Unfortunately, due to various internal problems or real-time obstructions, the Digital Crown may not function as it should in some conditions.

Follow the steps below to fix the problem relating to the Digital Crown;

- **Remove Obstructions**: Just like cleaning and maintaining your Apple Watch, the Digital Crown may be subjected to resistance, dirt, and dust that might have found its way into its crevices. Aside from making use of a damp cloth to clean, switch the Apple Watch off and then attempt running the Digital Crown under fresh water. Keep on pressing and turning the Digital Crown and clean thoroughly when you are through. Switch on the Apple Watch once more and see if it works.
- **Restart your Apple Watch**: If your Apple Watch is suffering from an internal bug, you can attempt to restart it. Since the Digital Crown is unavailable, you will have to tap and hold the Side Button until the Sliders show. Touch the Power Off Slider and move it to the right. Once your Apple Watch starts again, check if your Digital Crown is now working.
- **Reset your Apple Watch**: if the steps above do not do justice to the problem, you may have to reset your Apple Watch entirely. This will erase all data and your Apple Watch will go back to its default factory settings. On your Apple Watch, locate Settings, General, Reset, and choose **Erase All Content and Settings**. Ensure you have backed up your Apple Watch before embarking on this reset journey.

Apps won't download

With the use of your Apple Watch, you can download many applications from the App Store. These programs can help to bring improvement of system functionality or they can also tailor your device to certain needs. That being said, problems can still arise while the installation is ongoing which can stop your download progress.

Below are the various things you can consider in fixing this problem;

- **Connectivity issues**: Most download failures are often related to failure in internet connection. Ensure that you are in the range of the network and that your Apple Watch and iPhone both have access to the internet.
- **Install one app at a time**: if you are attempting to install more than just one application simultaneously, this can stop the installation process as your device

becomes overwhelmed or becomes constricted by the limits of your network. Hence, attempt downloading each application each application individually prior to going on to the next.

- **Automatic App Install:** By default, the applications on your iPhone that are also on watchOS will instantly download and install onto your Apple Watch Home Screen. If you are awaiting a download and it has not shown yet, the Automatic App install setting may be switched off. If you would like to switch it on again. Launch the Watch Application on your iPhone, choose My Watch followed by General, and toggle Automatic App install.

- **Check storage space and restart your devices:** if none of the above solves the problem and you notice you still have quite an amount of storage left you can then consider restarting your Apple Watch and paired iPhone. This may rest the connection and take off any software-related issues that may be causing the error.

Keeping Your WatchOS Up to Date

Each watch OS brings about new tools, fixes, and features, hence there is a need for you to ensure that your Apple Watch is always up to date. In most cases, an update will help with solving many problems. Anytime there is an update, you will get a notification on your smartwatch. Upon confirmation of the update, it installs instantly. If there is a need for you to manually install an update on your Apple Watch, follow the directions below to get to know how to do it. The easiest way to manually install an update is from your paired iPhone. You may be asked to insert your passcode to complete the installation. **Your device will restart instantly when the process has been completed.**

- Launch the **Watch app** on your paired iPhone and touch the **My Watch tab.**
- Touch **General**, then choose **Software Update.**
- If an update is needed, move down to it touch **Install,** and then follow the prompts on the screen.

You can also choose to update your watch without your iPhone with you. Connect your Apple Watch to Wi-Fi, position it on its charger, and follow the steps below. Ensure that the device is still charging as the updates continue. It will restart on its own when it is completed.

- Launch the **Settings application on your Apple Watch.**
- Touch **General, then touch Software Update.**

- **Your device will instantly scan for updates that are available.**
- If a software update is available, touch the I**nstall option.**

Resolving Critical Issues: Resetting and Restoring

There are times when you might have a need to solve a very critical issue as regards the use of your Apple Watch and the only way out will be to either reset or restore your watch. Issues ranging from network glitches to screen freezing, etc. are worth you having to reset or restore your Apple Watch.

Follow the set of instructions below to restart your Apple Watch;

- **Turn off your Apple Watch**: Tap and **hold the side button** until the sliders are being displayed then touch the **restart icon,** then move the Power Off slider to the right side.
- **Turn on your Apple Watch:** Hold **down the side button until the Apple logo is shown.**

It is worth noting that you cannot restart your Apple Watch while your watch is being charged.

Restart the paired iPhone

- **Turn off your iPhone**: Tap and hold **down the side button and a volume button**, then move the slider to the right side. You can also choose to go to **Settings > General > Shutdown.**

- **Turn on your iPhone**: Hold down **the side or top button until the Apple logo is displayed.**

Force Apple Watch to restart

If you cannot switch off your Apple Watch or if the problem you were experiencing still persists, there may be a need for you to force your Apple Watch to restart. Ensure that this should be your last resort and should be done only when you are unable to restart your Apple Watch by the process outlined above. To force restart, hold down **the side button and the Digital Crown at the same time for a minimum of ten seconds, until the Apple logo is being displayed.**

Restore Apple Watch from a backup

By default, when you pair your Apple Watch with your iPhone your Watch gets backed up to your iPhone instantly and you can choose to restore it from a stored backup. Apple Watch backups are usually included when you back up your iPhone either to the cloud or to your Mac or PC. If your backups are saved in iCloud, you are unable to see the information contained in them.

Backup and restore Apple Watch

- **Back up your Apple Watch:** When your Watch is paired with an iPhone, Apple Watch content is backed up nonstop to the iPhone. If you then unpair the devices, a backup will be done first.
- **Restore your Apple Watch from a backup**: If you pair your Apple Watch with the same iPhone once more, or you get a new Apple Watch, you can make a choice of Restoring from the Backup and choosing a saved backup on your iPhone.

An Apple Watch that is managed by a member of a family also backs up directly to the iCloud account of the family member when the watch is connected to a source of power and a Wi-Fi network. If you would like to disable iCloud backups for that watch, launch the S**ettings application on the managed Apple Watch**, locate **the account name > iCloud Backups, and then switch off iCloud Backups.**

Longevity Tips: Maintenance and Care Best Practices

For you to ensure that you are able to make use of your Apple Watch for many years, it is best you strictly adhere to the safety and maintenance instructions contained in this section.

It covers all the major important parts of your Apple Watch that need to be handled with care.

- **Handling:** Ensure that you handle your Apple Watch with care. Apple Watch has various sensitive electronic parts that can get easily damaged if dropped, burned, punctured, or even crushed. Apple Watch cases that are made of ceramic may chip or even crack if dropped or if it is subjected to a forceful impact. Do not use a damaged Apple Watch like one whose screen is cracked or case is cracked, one with visible liquid intrusion, or a damaged band, as this may lead to you sustaining an injury. Also, ensure that you stay clear of exposure to either dust or sand.
- **Repairing:** Ensure you do not open your Apple Watch and do not make any attempt to fix the Watch yourself. Disassembling your Apple Watch can lead to it

getting damaged, it can bring about loss in water resistance, and it may also lead to you having injury. If your Apple Watch is damaged or malfunctions, the best thing for you to do is to get across to Apple or an Apple Authorized Service Provider.

- **Battery**: Do not consider replacing your Apple Watch battery by yourself as this can lead to you damaging the battery, which can also lead to overheating and injury. The lithium-ion battery in the Apple Watch must be serviced only by Apple or any of their authorized service providers. You may also get a replacement Apple Watch when you place an order for a new battery. Batteries ought to be recycled or disposed of separately from any household waste. Ensure that you do not incinerate the battery.

- **Distraction**: Making use of Apple Watch in certain circumstances can lead to distraction and might also lead to a dangerous situation, for instance ensuring you are not reading a text message when you are driving a car. Observe various rules that restrict or hinder the use of mobile devices.

- **Navigation maps:** Maps, directions, and any location-dependent application rely heavily on data services. These data services are usually subject to change and may not be available in all places which means that the use of maps and any location-dependent application may not be available in all areas. Some Maps features have a need for Location Services. Take a comparison of the information offered on Apple Watch to your locality and defer to signs that are posted to solve any issue that may arise. Desist from the usage of these services while getting involved in activities that need your total attention. Ensure you are always in full compliance with posted signs as well as the laws and regulations that guide the areas where you are making use of the Apple Watch.

- **Charging**: Charge the Apple Watch with the use of an Apple Watch magnetic charging accessor and an Apple-compatible power adapter. It is worth noting that each of these accessories is usually sold differently. You can also choose to charge the Apple Watch with other third-party adapters that are compliant with USB 2.0 or later and with applicable country rules and regulations as well as international and regional safety standards.

The use of damaged cables or chargers, or charging when there is little moisture can lead to fire, electric shock, or complete damage to your Apple Watch or other property that may be in the same place as the Apple Watch. When you are making use of the Apple Watch magnetic charging accessory with a power adapter for the charging of your Apple device, ensure that the cable or dock is completely inserted into the power adapter prior to plugging the adapter into a power outlet. It is quite important to protect the Apple Watch, the Apple Watch magnetic charging accessory, and also the power adapter in an area that is well-ventilated when in use while it's charging.

- **Prolonged heat exposure**: Apple Watch and all of its charging accessories comply with the need for surface temperature limits that are stated by applicable country regulations and international and regional safety standards. Nevertheless, even within these limits, when there is contact with warm surfaces for a long period of time, it might lead to discomfort or even an injury. The Apple Watch as well as its accessories are usually quite warm when plugged into a source of power. The use of cellular on your Apple Watch Series 9 can also lead to your device feeling warm. Ensure you try to avoid situations where your skin comes in contact with the Apple Watch when they are plugged in. For instance, while the Apple Watch is being charged, ensure you do not lay on it or its power accessories; neither should you place them under a blanket, or a pillow. When you are wearing your watch and you notice an absurd hotness please take it off and turn it off, then leave it to cool for some minutes before you decide to wear it again.

- **Hearing loss:** Listening to sound at a volume that is extremely high can lead to damage to your hearing aids. Background noise, as well as prolonged exposure to high volume levels, can make sounds look as though they are quieter than they are supposed to be. Switch on audio playback and then check the volume prior to inserting a Bluetooth-connected headset in your ear. If you would like to prevent possible hearing damage, ensure you do not listen at a very high volume level over a long period of time.

- **Radiofrequency interference**: Ensure you observe any signs and notices that hinder the use of electronic devices. Although Apple Watch and Apple Watch magnetic charging accessories are created, tested, and produced in such a way that they obey all regulations that cover the use of radio frequency emissions. Ensure you unplug the Watch magnetic accessories and switch them off when you are in an area where its use is prohibited like when you are traveling in an aircraft, or when you are asked to get this done by the respective authorities.

- **Cleaning and care**: Ensure you keep your Apple Watch clean and away from moisture at all times. Clean and dry your Apple Watch, the band, and your skin after every workout session or heavy sweating. Ensure they are thoroughly cleaned and dry if they have been exposed to any form of moisture at any point in time. Also ensure you clean your Apple Watch whenever it comes in contact with anything like dirt, acids, or liquid, including anything that can lead to you having skin irritation like sweat, salt water, soapy water, insect repellant, sunscreen oil, etc

- **Use buttons, Digital Crown, connectors, and ports**: Ensure you refrain from applying too much pressure to a button or the Digital Crown on the Apple Watch or forcing a charging connector into a port as this can lead to damage that is not covered under the warranty that comes with your watch. If the connectors and port are unable to join with ease it simply means they are not a match. Be on the lookout for possible obstructions and ensure that they are a match for one another. Certain usage patterns can also play a major part in the fraying or breaking of cables. The cable connected to a charging unit, like any other metal wire or cable, is subject to getting weak or brittle if it is continually bent at the same place. Ensure you regularly check your connectors and ports to ensure that they are in perfect condition.

Activity

1. What are the common glitches you may experience with the use of your Apple watch and how best can you fix them?
2. Reset and Restore your Apple Watch.
3. Enumerate various means by which you can take good care of your watch.

CHAPTER 1
UNLOCKING HIDDEN POTENTIALS
Advanced Siri Commands and Shortcuts

With the use of Siri, you can do tasks and also get answers right on your Apple Watch. For instance, use Siri to translate what you say into a different language, identify a song, and also provide an instant Shazam result, or, after you ask a general question, show the first few search results and also a little excerpt from each page. All you have to do is touch Open Page to see the page on Apple Watch. Attempt making use of Siri to do various things that oftentimes take you some steps before you can get them done. It is worth noting that Siri is not available in all regions hence not everyone will be able to have access to this unique service.

Below are some of the commands you can get done with the use of Siri;

- Start a 30-minute outdoor run.
- Open the Sleep application.
- Open Settings
- What song is this?
- What causes rainbows?
- What are the things I can ask you?

To make a Siri request, do any of the following below;

- Raise your wrist and talk into your Apple Watch. If you would like to switch off the Raise to Speak features, launch the Settings application on your Apple Watch, **touch Siri then switch off Raise to Speak.**
- Say "Hey Siri" or just "Siri" then say your request. If you would like to switch off Ask Siri, launch the Settings application on your Apple Watch, touch **Siri, touch Listen for "Siri" or "Hey Siri"**

- Then choose **Off.**
- Touch and hold the Digital Crown until you get to see the listening sign, then say your request. If you would like to switch off the Press Digital Crown feature, launch the Settings application on your Apple Watch, touch Siri, and then switch off Press Digital Crown.

To reply to a question from Siri or to keep a conversation with Sir, hold down the Digital Crown and speak. Siri can speak responses to you as it does on iOS, iPadOS, and macOS. If you are making use of a Bluetooth headset or speakers connected to your Apple Watch, you can also hear Siri via it. Note also that to make use of Siri, it must be connected to the internet. Cellular charges may also apply depending on your carrier.

Choose how Siri responds

Siri can speak responses on your Apple Watch. Launch the Settings application on your Apple Watch, touch Siri Responses, and then make your preferred choice from the following;

- **Always On**: With this choice, Siri speaks responses even when your Apple Watch is in silent mode.
- **Control with Silent Mode:** With this choice, the responses from Siri are silenced when your Apple Watch is configured to silent mode.

- **Headphones Only**: With this choice, Siri will only speak its responses when your Apple Watch is connected to Bluetooth headphones.

If you would like to alter the language and voice used for Siri, launch the Settings application on your Apple Watch, touch Siri, and then touch Language or Siri Voice. When you touch Siri Voice you can make a choice of a different variety or voice.

Display captions and transcriptions of your Siri requests

Your Apple Watch is able to show the captions and transcriptions from Siri of your Siri requests and responses. If you would like to later either option, launch the Settings application on your Apple Watch, touch **Siri, touch Siri responses, move down**, and then switch **Always Show Siri Captions and Always Show Speech on or off.**

Type to Siri and Siri Pause Time

If for any reason you happen to have any form of difficulty speaking, you can choose to type Siri requests or ask that Siri wait a little longer for you to finish talking.

- Launch the **Settings application on your Apple Watch.**
- Locate **Accessibility > Siri**

- **And then switch on Type to Siri**
- If you would like Siri to wait a little more for you to finish talking, touch Longer or Longest beneath Siri Pause Time.

Delete Siri history

When you make use of Siri or dictation, your requests are saved for about 6 months on Apple servers to help make Siri's responses to you much better. Your requests are linked with a random identifier, not with your Apple ID or email address. You can choose to delete these interactions from the server at any time of your choice.

- Launch the **Settings application on your Apple Watch.**
- Touch Siri, touch **Siri History**

- **And then touch Delete Siri History.**

Announce Notifications

Siri is able to read out incoming notifications from various applications without you having to unlock your iPhone when you are making use of supported AirPods and Beats headphones.

Turn on Announce notifications

- Place your paired headphones in your ears, based on the type of headphones you are using.
- Pair **them with an Apple Watch.**

- Launch the **Settings application on your Apple Watch.**
- Locate **Siri > Announce Notifications, and then switch on Announce Notifications.**

It is worth noting also that Siri is able to read your unread notifications in the Notification Center either via the Apple Watch speaker or through headphones connected via Bluetooth. All you have to say is "Read my notifications '.

Choose applications for notifications

You can make a choice of the applications that are permitted to announce notifications.

- Place your paired headphones in or on your ears, based on the type of headphones you are making use of.
- Launch the **Settings application on your Apple Watch.**
- Locate **Siri > Announce Notifications.** Navigate **down, then choose the applications you would like to get audio notifications from.**

Reply to a message

Say something like "Reply that's great news" Siri will repeat what you have just said, and then request confirmation prior to sending your reply. If you would like to send replies without a need to wait for confirmation, launch the Settings application on your Apple Watch, locate **Siri > Announce Notifications, move to the lower part, and then switch on Reply without confirmation**.

Stop Siri from reading a notification

You can choose to get any of the following done;

- Say something like "Stop or "Cancel".
- Tap the **Digital Crown (AirPods Max)**

It is worth noting that while you are listening to a notification, you can switch the Digital Crown to alter the volume.

- Tap **either Force Sensor (AirPods and AirPods 3rd generation).**

- Tap y**our AirPods (2nd generation) twice.**
- Take off one of your AirPods (AirPods and AirPods 2nd and 3rd generation).

If you did not switch on Announce Notifications when you set up your AirPods, launch the Settings application on your Apple Watch, locate Siri > Announce Notifications, and then switch on Announce Notifications.

Announce calls with Siri on Apple Watch

Siri is able to announce calls and notifications from applications like Messages on supported headphones. Announce Calls also works with supported third-party applications.

- Launch the **Settings application on your Apple Watch.**
- Touch **Siri, and then switch on Announce Calls.**
- When you get a call, the caller will be identified, and when you are asked if you would like to respond to the call simply say "yes" to accept the call or "no" to decline the call.

Homekit Integration and Smart Home Control

The Home app offers a very secure way to manage HomeKit-enabled accessories, like lights, locks, smart TVs, thermostats, window shades, and smart plugs. You can also send and receive Intercom messages on supported devices and see the video streams of HomeKit Secure Video cameras. With the use of your Apple Watch, all your controls will come directly from your wrist. The first time you open the Home app on your iPhone, the setup assistant will help with the creation of a home. Once that has been done, you will then be able to define rooms, include HomeKit-enabled accessories, and design scenes. Accessories, scenes, and rooms that you include on your iPhone can be found on your Apple Watch.

View your home status

Open the Home application, then navigate to display the following sections;

- **Cameras**: Video from up to about four cameras shows close to the top of the display. Touch a camera to have a view of its video stream.

- **Categories**: Touch your preferred category like Lights, Security, Climate, Speakers, or Water to display all related accessories on one screen, organized by room. A number showing close to a category signifies an accessory that could make use of your attention; for instance, the temperature registered by your thermostat for an unlocked front door. Just touch a button to manage the accessory or get to learn more.

You can swiftly manage all the lights and speakers in your home. For instance, if more than one lights are on, touch the Lights category, then touch All Lights Off. In the Speakers category, touch Pause All to pause any speaker that might be playing.

- **Relevant accessories**: The relevant scenes and accessories for that moment will be displayed close to the top of the screen. For instance, a coffee maker may show up in the morning and be replaced by your bedside lamp at night.

Control smart home accessories and scenes

If you would like to manage an accessory in the Home application, get any of the following done;

- **Turn an accessory on or off:** Touch **the accessory**-for instance a light, or if you would like to unlock a compatible lock, a home key.
- **Adjust an accessory's settings**: Touch **the more options** for an accessory. Touch the X icon to go back to the list of accessories. The controls that are available are based on the type of accessory. For instance, with certain light bulbs, there are various controls for both brightness and altering colors. Move left to see more controls.
- **Control favorite accessories, scenes, or accessories in a room**: Touch the left arrow icon, choose **Favorites, Scenes, or a room, then touch a scene or an accessory, or touch more options to alter the accessory settings**.
- **View a camera's video stream**: On the Home screen, touch a camera. If you have more than four of them, touch **the + button to have a view of all your cameras, then touch a camera.**

You can also touch a room with a camera in it, and then touch the camera. If you would like to run a scene, launch the Home app on your Apple Watch, then touch the scene.

View a different home

If you happen to have more than just one home set up, you can the exact one you would like to view on your Apple Watch. Launch the Home application on your Apple Watch, touch the left arrow icon twice, and then choose a home.

Unlocking the Power of Watch Complications

In the context of the Apple Watch, a complication does not mean something complicated. Apple here does not mean that you will have to panic or get worried over a difficulty or something, it is simply making reference to the Swiss watch industry. The language used is created to bring up imagery of traditional mechanical timepieces like that of Rolex is Breitling, as against smartwatches. In reality complications from Apple simply mean widgets. With Apple Watch complications, you are able to alter elements displayed on the watch face. There is a need for you to Force Touch display and move to the customization section where you will locate the complications that are provided. This feature has also been opened to third-party developers following Watch OS 2. These customizable widgets help to show useful information straight to the watch face. It also offers rapid access to diverse application data and features without a need for the user to open the corresponding applications. These complications can show diverse data which includes market prices, activity progress, weather updates, calendar events, and lots more.

Below are examples of some of the complications;

- **Pedometer ++**: This is a user-friendly fitness application that has been created to keep track of daily steps and also promote an active lifestyle. Its simple interface and specificity in step-counting algorithm offer an easy way to keep track of your physical activity and also configure fitness goals. The application provides insightful data like distance covered, amount of calories burned, and active time, enabling you to check your progress over time. This app also offers integration with Apple Health, giving room for seamless synchronization of your step across various devices.
- **AutoSleep Track Sleep on Watch**: AutoSleep Track can be described as a comprehensive sleep-tracking application created for Apple Watch users. It has a

very friendly user interface with innovative features that help you get an idea of your sleep patterns and also improve your overall sleep quality. The application instantly knows when you fall asleep and when you are awake, removing the need for you to manually start and stop tracking. It offers comprehensive details about your sleep time, quality of sleep, heart rate, and lots more. Apart from all of the listed features, it has so many other useful features like blood oxygen measurement, respiratory rate measurements, Siri voice commands, integration with the home kit and health app, and lots more.

- **CARROT Weather**: this is a very unique and engaging weather application that offers accurate forecasts and real-time weather updates. Its witty and humorous personality provides quite a refreshing twist to your daily weather experience. The application has a wide range of features which include hyperlocal weather data, customizable widgets, and detailed radar maps. It also offers severe weather alerts, ensuring that you are well-informed and ready for any form of upcoming weather events. The application has augmented reality that enables the creation of news and filmy-style weather reports.

- **HeartWatch**: If you are an athlete, one who is included with being fit or you are simply just conscious about your heart, HeartWatch is a very useful application for tracking and optimizing your heart rate that helps with gaining valuable insights into your cardiovascular health. The application offers accurate and real-time heart rate measurements, enabling you to check the activity of your heart all through the day. It also helps with the provision of customizable heart rate alerts, ensuring that you are well informed if your heart rate exceeds or falls below specified thresholds. You can keep an eye on morning health information, and fitness habits, check out your daily workout, and lots more. The application enables you to make notes and journals to take note of very important information like temperature, blood pressure, and body fat.

- **Tile**: this is the best application for keeping track of your belongings like keys, wallets, bags, and lots more. The application enables you to locate near and far-off misplaced items with ease with the help of a Bluetooth tracker. You are also able to locate your lost phone; all you have to do is tap the tile app to bring about a ring on the phone. This app can be used with other apps like Amazon Alexa, Google Assistant, and many other applications by syncing the tile app to activate the smart home feature. You don't have to worry even if your tile has been lost, all you have to do is add a contact number, and you will be immediately notified when anyone scans your QR code.

- **Fantastical Calendar**: this is a very powerful calendar application that helps to simplify your scheduling and also helps to ensure that you remain organized. Its amazing interface enables you to seamlessly design events, set reminders, and manage your daily, weekly, and monthly plans. The application provides features like natural language input, wherein you are able to type or speak details of your event and it will immediately understand and get the event designed accordingly. Fantastical Calendar also syncs with well-known services like Google Calendar, iCloud, and Exchange, making sure of seamless syncing across all of your devices.
- Motivation: everyone has a need for positive thoughts and motivations that can help to uplift one's mood in order to keep pressing on. This unique application provides a daily dose of inspiration directly to your watch. Each day, users with this app get a new quote that brings about positive thinking, self-improvement, and perseverance. You can also alter font colors, filter by specific category, or add the application as a home screen widget for ease of access.

Activity

1. With the use of Siri, command your watch to do certain things.
2. Control your home with the use of your watch.

Conclusion

The Apple wearable Series 9 adds new capabilities to the top-selling wearable in the world while also setting an important environmental milestone. With the redesigned S9 SiP, which improves performance and capabilities, the brighter display, faster on-device Siri, which can now access and log health data, Precision Finding for iPhone, and more, the Apple Watch Series 9 is more potent than ever. WatchOS 10 on the Apple Watch Series 9 includes updated apps, the new Smart Stack, fresh watch faces, improved cycling and hiking features, and resources to assist mental health.

The brand-new S9 SiP in the Apple Watch Series 9 is powered by specially designed Apple silicon. The new double-tap gesture and on-device Siri with the ability to access and log health data safely and securely are just two of the system-wide upgrades and brand-new capabilities that Apple's most potent watch chip has to offer. When compared to Apple

Watch Series 8, the new 4-core Neural Engine in Apple Watch Series 9 can process machine learning tasks up to twice as quickly. The S9 SiP's power efficiency enables the Apple Watch Series 9 to retain an 18-hour battery life throughout the day. Apple Watch is easy to use because of innovations like the Digital Crown and Taptic Engine, as well as movements like tapping, swiping, raising the wrist, and covering the microphone. Users can quickly navigate the Apple Watch Series 9 with just one hand and without touching the touchscreen thanks to a new double-tap gesture. Also, on the Apple Watch Series 9, users may swiftly and efficiently carry out many of the most popular actions by tapping their index finger and thumb together twice.

INDEX

B

J

K

L

M

T

Y

Z

89693248R00131